Fort Hunter Mansion *and Park*

A Guide

Carl A. Dickson

STACKPOLE BOOKS

Published by
STACKPOLE BOOKS
5067 Ritter Road
Mechanicsburg, PA 17055
www.stackpolebooks.com

Printed in the United States of America

10 9 8 7 6 5 4 3 2 1

FIRST EDITION

Cover design by Tracy Patterson
All illustrations are from the collection of Fort Hunter Mansion and Park, courtesy of the Dauphin County Commissioners, unless otherwise noted.
Front Cover: Houseparty in honor of Helen and John Reily's third wedding anniversary, 1890.
Back Cover: Farmhands in front of stone stable, c. 1900. John Reily, with prized pig, named "Jim," outside centennial barn, c. 1915.

Library of Congress Cataloging-in-Publication Data

Dickson, Carl A.
   Fort Hunter Mansion and Park : a guide / Carl A. Dickson–1st ed.
     p. cm.
   ISBN 0-8117-2757-2
   1. Fort Hunter Mansion and Park (Harrisburg, Pa.)–Guidebooks. 2. Harrisburg Region (Pa.)–Buildings, structures, etc.–Guidebooks. 3. Fort Hunter Mansion and Park (Harrisburg, Pa.)–History. 4. Harrisburg Region (Pa.)–History. 5. Fort Hunter Mansion and Park (Harrisburg, Pa.)–Pictorial works. I. Title.

F159.H3 D53 2002
974.8'18–dc21
                                                        2001042993

Contents

Introduction

Located two miles north of Harrisburg, the capital of Pennsylvania, on the bank of the tranquil Susquehanna River, Fort Hunter Mansion and Park offers visitors the rare opportunity to experience three hundred years of the American past on one property. With a history spanning Native Americans, frontier settlers, a British fortification site, an early plantation, Victorian country life, and finally, an early museum, Fort Hunter exhibits a surprising breadth of historic characters and events. The stories of these people are told in elegant surroundings, with the help of an abundance of original artifacts and buildings. Educational programs, exhibits, special events, and guided tours throughout the year facilitate the interpretation of the people of Fort Hunter.

This forty-acre park, nestled between mountains and river, contains ten historic structures, gardens, a cemetery, the Pennsylvania Canal, a museum store, a small conference center, picnic pavilions, playground equipment, play fields, a fishing stream, and nature trails. Fort Hunter is owned by Dauphin County, managed by the Dauphin County Parks and Recreation Department and the Board of Trustees for Fort Hunter, and supported by the Friends of Fort Hunter, Inc.

The Frontier and the Fort, 1650–1787

At a point where the majestic Susquehanna River cuts a mile-wide swath through the Appalachian Mountains, both water and earth uniquely converge at Fort Hunter. This unusually picturesque meeting of geography leaves little flat land for settlement. Because of these physical constraints, the relatively confined lands of Fort Hunter have a long and varied history.

Accepted geologic thought suggests that as the earth evolved, the pressure of surface plates against each other was so great as to push the edges of the plates skyward, creating mountains. When it rained, water naturally moved with gravity down the sides of these mountains and into the valleys, creating creeks that flow into great rivers and move toward the sea. Typically, then, mountain ranges developed first, and parallel streams and rivers followed. Oddly, at Fort Hunter, the river runs perpendicular to and cuts through the mountain range.

The large mountains and wide river at Fort Hunter create natural barriers. Because of the size of these barriers, human interactions here naturally took

The Fort Hunter lands are shown sandwiched between the mountains and the river in this aerial view.

place on the relatively small plot of flat land. It has been in continual use from man's earliest existence in the area through today.

The Indians were the earliest humans known to have inhabited this area. Initially they lived a nomadic life, hunting with spears and traveling the region. As time progressed, specific family territories developed, and about one thousand years ago, the Indians in this area began to settle in villages and cultivate

Here the Blue or Kittatinny Mountain of the Allegheny region of the Appalachian range crosses the Susquehanna.

Susquehannock Indians are portrayed as large, elegant people in this often reproduced sketch from the notebook of John Smith, c. 1608.

dians became more dependent on these tools and looked for opportunities to trade for them. As an agrarian people, the Indians had rich cornfields, but the settlers were not interested in trading hoes, kettles, and guns for corn. Instead, fur, fashionable in Europe, proved to be a favorable commodity, as well as a highly profitable one to the white traders. So the Indians turned away from their agricultural lifestyle and back to their ancestors' life of hunting—not for food, but for pelts to trade.

The Susquehannocks' location on the lower Susquehanna was advantageous for fur trade with European settlers on the Delaware and Chesapeake Bays. As areas quickly became overhunted, however, hunting boundaries expanded into the territories of other tribes. Clashes inevitably broke out. The destruction of the Susquehannocks in 1675 during the Beaver Wars, a fight between tribes for the right to hunt and trade in certain areas, opened the way for the Delaware, or Lenape, to make settlements on the Susquehanna and to supplant their former neighbors in the fur trade. These are the people most identified as Pennsylvania Indians.

As pressure from settlement continued, the Indians moved west, and tribes began to split up as a result of war or disease. Displaced Indians from various tribes, including Shawnee, Nanticoke, Tuscarora, Conoy, and Tutelo, began to settle this area of the Susquehanna with the permission of the northern Iroquois Confederacy, or Five Nations.

During this great migration of Indians through Pennsylvania, especially in

the ground. This sophisticated, agrarian lifestyle allowed them more time to think, interact, and develop communities.

The earliest Indians known in this Pennsylvania region were the Susquehannocks, also called the Minquas or Andastes. In his book *Indians in Pennsylvania*, Paul Wallace sets the Blue Mountain, north of Fort Hunter, as a convenient boundary for various tribes. He places the Susquehannocks south of the mountain by the beginning of the seventeenth century. Wallace describes the tribes as a refined, well-organized, military people living in stockaded villages headed by a chief.

As exposure to the metal tools of incoming white settlers increased, the In-

Modest mills were scattered in the Pennsylvania countryside in the 1700s.

the late 1600s and early 1700s, represen-
tatives from all of these tribes may have
passed through or stopped on the land
that would be Fort Hunter. The conflu-
ence of Fishing Creek and the Susquehanna River, along the base of Blue
Mountain, provided a natural geographic
landmark and meeting place. Many spear

points and other stone artifacts have
been found at Fort Hunter over the years.

According to tradition, the earliest
known white settler in the Fort Hunter
region was Benjamin Chambers. In
1872, local historian A. Boyd Hamilton,
whose assertions are difficult to confirm,
wrote that "the four brothers who came

to Fort Hunter were Presbyterians, and came from Ulster Ireland, about 1723." Benjamin, James, Joseph, and Robert Chambers arrived on the banks of the Susquehanna in about 1725 or 1726. Hamilton writes:

In 1725–26 a title under the fashion of that period was acquired [by Chambers] "at the mouth of Fishing Creek," for one thousand acres, from Robert Hunter, a straggling white trader, who had wedded "Mrs. Corondowana alias Mrs. Montour," a chieftainess of the Conoys, "about a year and a half" before, April, 1723, of which marriage loud complaint was made to "Pat'ck Gordon, Esq., Lt. Gov'r, and the Coun'l." This transaction on the borders made a commotion at the council board of the Penn family and therefore fixes, with reasonable certainty, the location of the Chambers family. Subsequently the provincial authorities confirmed all that had taken place, through land office forms, about 1733–37. A few hundred yards from what afterward was the fort a mill was built about 1736.

It was not until October 1736 that the Penn Proprietorship, through treaty with the Iroquois, obtained title to these lands located south of Blue Mountain. If, as was so often the case, people settled on this property without the consent of the proprietorship, then Hamilton's paper would suggest that Robert Hunter was the first settler at Fort Hunter. Yet it is unclear how "a title under the fashion of that period" was acquired by Chambers from Hunter when the land was not yet owned by the Penn Proprietorship. The earlier dates would, however, corroborate that settlement often occurred without regard to ownership. The constant influx of settlers left local Indians with a sense of powerlessness. They were constantly harassed by the settlers, and many departed from the area. The eventual extinction of fur-bear-

ing species in overhunted areas made the decision to move imperative.

Benjamin and James Chambers moved on as well. They settled in what is now Franklin County, in an area then known as Falling Springs, later named Chambersburg, after the family. Brothers Joseph and Robert, however, are said to have remained at Fort Hunter.

Hamilton continued:

In 1746 David Brainerd, on his mission from New England to convert the Indians on the Susquehanna, got a taste of the quality of the frontiersmen on this locality. He notes in his journal: "Rode this day, August 20 to one Chambers's upon the Susquehanna, and there lodged. Was much afflicted in the evening with an ungodly crew, drinking, swearing," and so on.

Conrad Weiser was an agent for the Penn Proprietors, appointed to negotiate with the Indians. He worked closely with the Iroquois chief, Shikellamy, who had been appointed by his people to represent the confederacy of Indian nations. Hamilton noted an excerpt from a 1747 document: "Conrad Weiser and Shickelemy in conference at the house of Joseph Chambers in Paxton." The result of this interview was that Weiser reported, "I am satisfied that the Inguns have just reason to complain at the behavior of some of our people."

Locally, this demeanor contributed to the events leading up to the French and Indian War and the development of Fort Hunter as a link in a chain of fortifications constructed by the British to protect their interests. But more important and on a larger scale were the animosities among the French, Dutch, Spanish, and English nations, which were competing for trade markets and Colonial raw materials. Despite the huge size and plentiful resources of North America, western

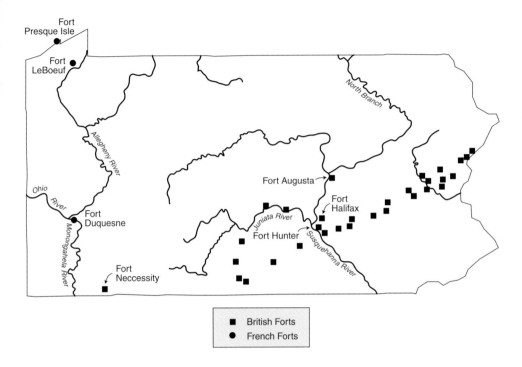

The British built a chain of forts throughout Pennsylvania. Fort Hunter was located at a pivotal juncture for both north-south and east-west traffic.

European nations were unwilling to share it. Conflict over these resources was constant both here and abroad. The fur trade was particularly volatile.

The conflicts that developed, collectively known as the French and Indian Wars, consisted of four phases: King William's War (1689–97), Queen Anne's War (1702–13), King George's War (1744–45), and the French and Indian War (1754–63). Fort Hunter was built and played a role in the last chapter of this series, the French and Indian War.

The French, almost consistently the provocateurs, had moved down through Canada and built a string of barrier forts south from Lake Erie along the Pennsylvania line and the Allegheny River Valley: Fort Presque Isle, Fort Le Boeuf, Fort Venango, and Fort Duquesne (where the Allegheny and Monongahela Rivers join

to form the Ohio at present-day Pittsburgh). The enraged English sent an army from the continent to try to take Fort Duquesne from the French. General Braddock was in command, and a young George Washington was one of his aides.

On July 9, 1755, after a long and arduous march across Pennsylvania and just ten miles short of their destination, the French and Indians ambushed the English. Though greatly outnumbered, the French and their Indian compatriots brutalized the very formal fighting English. Over nine hundred of the twelve hundred English troops were killed or wounded. This battle, in which General Braddock lost his life, became known as Braddock's Defeat. The Indians, armed by the French, angry, and, after their recent victory, fearless, began to bathe the frontier in blood. After 150 years of

In 1787, John and Mary Garber sold the Fort Hunter lands to Archibald McAllister by this indenture.

being pushed back by white advances, they began to push forward by attacking individual farms, killing or capturing whomever they found, burning any structures, and performing other acts of startling brutality.

The English, in reaction, began an effort to construct a supply and communications chain through the vast territory. A line of forts built along the mountains in strategic locations, such as waterways and the junction of important trails,

would serve to protect the scattered British colonists from attack. Local men patrolled between the individual forts in a confident, though often unsuccessful, attempt to create a cordon of safety.

The line of forts constructed or sponsored by the British spanned east to west from the Delaware River to the Susquehanna along both sides of Blue Mountain. Fort Hunter formed the western terminus of the east-west line at the Susquehanna, as well as the terminus to the forts to the north, such as Fort Halifax, near present-day Halifax, Pennsylvania, and Fort Augusta, at present-day Sunbury. The line of forts also continued west from Fort Hunter across the broad Susquehanna and down the Allegheny Mountain range. Fort Hunter was a central communications link in this chain as well as a lookout for travelers moving through the pass formed by the Susquehanna's path through the Alleghenies.

On the site that was to become Fort Hunter, in 1748, Joseph Chambers, the owner of the land, died intestate, or without a will. His widow, Catherine Chambers, married a man named Samuel Hunter. (It is not known whether he was related to the previously mentioned Robert Hunter.) As news of the Indian raids and massacres spread, the buildings, formerly known as Chambers' Mill and now called Hunter's Mill, were quickly fortified by their inhabitants as a stronghold.

The exact location of the fort is not known today. It was most likely a small, simple structure placed on the bluff overlooking the river in close proximity to the present-day Mansion House. This is the highest piece of ground for quite some distance in either direction on the bank of the river, affording excellent views of the waterway with no risk of flooding. What the structure looked like can be only guessed. Writings suggest that there was a dormitory outside the walls, as the fort itself was not large enough to house many people. Instead, it was a place for emergency protection, fitted with a small storehouse for supplies.

Very little mention is made of Fort Hunter after July 1758. The scene of action had shifted, and the fort was readily abandoned.

In 1763, Pontiac's brutal rebellion caused settlers to mobilize quickly once again. The Fort Hunter–Hunter's Mill area was chosen as a rendezvous point for men and equipment before they proceeded to Fort Augusta. After the danger passed, the fort was once again abandoned and began to deteriorate. Though there is no record of its exact location or layout, its name remains tied to the land.

On June 3, 1766, with the threat of attack a recent memory, Samuel Hunter finally officially purchased the land of Fort Hunter. While long referred to as Hunter's Mill, and later Fort Hunter, ownership of the land itself was a legal knot. On that date, however, a detailed deed from the Penns conveyed 289 acres at a cost of £590.

A few days after the deed was filed, Samuel Hunter sold the entire tract to John and Mary Garber of Earl Township, Lancaster County, for the sum of £620. Little is known about them. They owned Fort Hunter for seventeen years, through the duration of the Revolutionary War, and sold the land in 1787 to Archibald McAllister for the large sum of £4,000.

The Building of
a Plantation,
1787–1870

Fort Hunter retains many physical remnants of Archibald McAllister's ownership, which began in May 1787. Under layers added by subsequent owners, McAllister's grand Federal-style Mansion of 1814, his Tavern House of c. 1810, an English-style barn, springhouse, icehouse, and dairy remain.

These solid buildings are constructed of stone and have weathered the tides of changing economies, as well as our culture's disregard for old buildings. This was clearly a prosperous area. The houses are large, with spacious hallways, six-foot-tall windows, and details stylish enough for more urban and sophisticated locales. Through these structures, McAllister speaks strongly about his place in society.

Portraits of Archibald and his wife, Elizabeth, painted in 1816, confirm a life of wealth and comfort at Fort Hunter. They depict Archbald as a lean, intelligent gentleman with receding gray hair, holding a book and glasses—proud symbols of an education that only a wealthy gentleman could afford—and Elizabeth as a plump woman, (what would now be considered overweight was then indicative of wealth), elegantly and conservatively dressed in brown satin. A family history written in 1898 by Mary Catherine McAllister, combined with additional details

Lancaster artist Jacob Eichholtz painted Archibald and Elizabeth McAllister in 1816.

learned through research, help create a clearer picture of Archibald McAllister and his life at Fort Hunter.

Archibald was born the fourth child, and second son, of Richard and Mary Dill McAllister on April 17, 1756. His father bought a large tract of land called "Digges' Choice" in 1764 and founded the town of McAllister, which is now known as Hanover in York County.

According to Mary Catherine McAllister, "The first record found of him is as a Captain of a Company in Colonel Hartley's Sixth Regiment of the Pennsylvania Line" during the Revolutionary War in 1777. "Though but 21 years of age, for gallantry, Gen. Washington, on the field presented him with a pair of silver mounted pistols." McAllister resigned his commission on November 19, 1777.

On April 9, 1778, he married Margaret Hays (b. April 24, 1761) and settled on a farm in Londonderry Township near present-day Hershey that had been willed to his wife through her deceased father's estate. She gave birth to a daughter, Mary Hays McAllister, who survived only seven days, dying on January 5, 1779. Tragically, Archibald's wife, Margaret, died five days later and was buried at Derry Church.

Because of the inheritance traditions of the day, and in spite of the brevity of the marriage, Archibald appears to have become the owner of his deceased father-in-law's 253-acre farm and the main beneficiary of the estate. The 1780 county "Register of Negro and Mulatto Slaves and Servants" lists that on September 11 Archibald had five slaves: Ned, aged 52; Isaac, 20; Sall, 14; Nance, 10; and Jem, 8. This would have been a substantial amount of responsibility for twenty-four-year-old Archibald.

On September 14, 1780, Archibald married Elizabeth Carson. Interestingly,

Elizabeth Carson, listed as a widow from Paxton Township and the owner of one slave, "Pompey, aged 14 years," had visited the registry office earlier that week.

Elizabeth was the only surviving daughter of John Carson and Mrs. Elizabeth (Wood) Gillespie. In 1743, John Carson had established a successful trading post on land located on the Susquehanna River about two miles south of Fort Hunter. His early history in the area and trading success made his family locally significant and another excellent marriage opportunity.

On December 21, 1781, Archibald and Elizabeth's first child was born— George Washington McAllister, named for the general under whom Archibald had served during the Revolutionary War. In August 1784, they had a second son, Thomas Gates McAllister. Amelia Mary was born on August 31, 1786, and Matilda Willis, on August 26, 1788. A third son, John Carson, born on September 21, 1790, would eventually become the owner of Fort Hunter. Richard, the couple's last child on record, was born on September 20, 1792.

The family genealogist, Mary Catherine McAllister, writes rather simply, "On May 6, 1785, [Archibald] removed to the farm of 150 acres, at Fort Hunter, on the Susquehanna river, six miles above Harrisburg, Pa."

The creation of Dauphin County in 1785, with nearby Harrisburg as its county seat, undoubtedly encouraged Archibald to purchase the aesthetically pleasing Fort Hunter property. The setting had the potential to be financially rewarding: Any travel north or south in that area had to pass through the Fort Hunter property, making it a natural crossroads and gathering spot—an ideal setting in which to generate income by offering services to travelers. Elizabeth likely was pleased with the location, too, as it was close to her father's large land holdings.

Archibald officially purchased the property from John and Mary Garber on February 24, 1787, paying £4,000 in gold and silver for the 331 acres. Local lore has long said that an old house and sawmill existed on the site when Archibald purchased it, possibly dating to the original settlement by the Chambers family; account books and the deed description support this idea. Over the next thirty years, Archibald continued to add to and subtract from his land holdings, as land speculation was a sensible investment.

From 1788 through 1807, Archibald received licenses from the government to run a tavern at Fort Hunter. Taverns played an integral role in the dissemination of information, providing a venue for important community interaction in what was at the time largely a farming nation. Information was exchanged verbally or through the written word, but few could read. A farmer and his family would come to Archibald's small village and, while waiting for grain to be ground or other business, could stop in the tavern, perhaps have a drink, but more importantly, enjoy social interaction with members of their surrounding community. Newspapers hanging on racks brought news of the world around them. If they could not read, there were always others to explain and discuss the politics and other goings-on of the surrounding country. Travelers could stay for a night or two in a few shared bedrooms on the second floor of the building.

Archibald also did a significant business distilling his own alcoholic beverages and selling them in cities, chiefly Philadelphia. A recipe for the making of "Cider Royal" is found between McAllister's memos of log purchases.

The tavern was only one of his many business interests. Others included sawmills and gristmills, selling sundries, and loaning cash. He sold such items as yarn, flour, whiskey, wheat, brandy, and lumber, including lath and "poplar for joists," but the majority of sales are listed as sundries.

Interestingly, in 1794, a Mr. McKinley made his mark to promise to deliver to the esteemed "Dr. Priestly in North Umberland" four barrels of apples on November 13 and three tierces of cider on November 28. Joseph Priestley was a scientist and theologian who resided in the town of Northumberland, about sixty miles north of Fort Hunter on the Susquehanna River, and is best known for his discovery of oxygen.

The Duke de La Rochefoucault-Liancourt, in his diary entries documenting his travels about America, said of Fort Hunter in 1796: "McAllister owns about 300 acres, about 120 cultivated. Price of lands near him is $8 for woodland: $50 for cleared. The houses, all of wood except the Inn, which stands on the Susquehanna and in the precincts of Fort Hunter, erected many years ago."

The 1798 Direct Tax or "glass tax" describes Archibald's improvements in detail, listing a two-story "Dwelling house" of stone and wood with fourteen windows containing 168 lights (windowpanes), a wooden kitchen, wooden smokehouse, stone springhouse, stone icehouse, and one-story wood tenant house occupied by Henry Keller. Another entry records 149 acres, a stone and wood barn, stone merchant mill, sawmill, stone still house, cider house, tenant houses occupied by Peter Junk and James Hays, an adjoining 119 acres of mountain land, and two slaves. All of this suggests a growing and bustling settlement.

The Pennsylvania capitol in Harrisburg, constructed in 1822.

Archibald's religious affiliation is typical for his background and the area. He is listed as a commissioner to raise £5,000 for the purpose of erecting the First Presbyterian Church of Harrisburg. The lot was purchased in 1804, and following the convention of the time, his account books show his pew fee paid into 1834.

An excerpt from the diary of Mrs. Hannah Haines, whose elegant home, Wyck, is located in Germantown, near Philadelphia, provides additional insight into the McAllisters at Fort Hunter.

1812, 6mo., 23d—Again commenced our journey [illegible] it was evening when we got to McAllister's a house of excellent accommodation, but found that they had given up keeping tavern, but politely requested us to alight, and after refreshing us with a nice dish of tea we retired to our chambers. 6mo., 24th— Rain—uncommon civility of the family; excellent library, most elegant tea set of china with fruit baskets, every piece was a different pattern of flowers and fruit of every variety fancifully arranged on a ground of the purest white. It was sent from an association of Moravians at Dresden to their Brethren settled in Bethlehem, but they considering it too expensive a luxury sold it for £40. Showed us a very ancient Bible in the English language, year 1534, also a very large carpet of their own manufactory equal to any import I ever saw.

This passage describes the elegant appointments at Fort Hunter and the refined hospitality of the McAllisters as appreciated by a cultivated lady. Clearly, Archibald was living the life of a comfortable country gentleman.

The local transfer of the Pennsylvania capital to Harrisburg in 1812 undoubtedly fortified Archibald's financial outlook for his Fort Hunter setting. By 1814, he felt secure enough in his economic situation that he built an ambitious stone addition to his earlier

This aqueduct was built to carry the Pennsylvania Canal over Fishing Creek on the property.

stone cabin. With eleven-foot ceilings on both the first and second stories, a finished third floor, and twelve rooms in all, the Mansion House stands on a bluff overlooking the expanse of the Susquehanna River to the west and McAllister's working community to the east. Fitted with a stylish entrance door complete with large fanlight and side-lights, a cantilevered spiral staircase ascending three floors, and a Palladian window on the second floor centered over the front door, this bright and airy home was the height of elegance, especially given its distance of six miles from the center of the fledgling city.

In 1818, English writer William Cobbett wrote:

My business not coming on, I went to a country tavern, hoping there to get a room to myself, in which to read my English papers, and sit down to writing. I am now at McAllisters tavern, situated at the foot of the first ridge of mountains: or rather, upon a little nook of land, close to the river, where the river has found a way through a break in the chain of mountains.

He goes on to say that he likes the tavernkeeper's wife because "she does not pester me with questions. Does not cram me with meat. Let's me eat and drink what I like, when I like, and gives me mugs of nice milk."

As his businesses prospered, Archibald's 1818 journals reflect increases in sales of whiskey, brandy, wine, "cherry," gin, and cider sold in gallons, quarts, pints, and gills. The sale of gills—a small quantity, four gills making a pint—would suggest that Archibald continued to run a tavern.

The death of Elizabeth on January 18, 1822, at age fifty-seven, undoubtedly was a difficult blow to McAllister. This, coupled with his own advancing age—he was now sixty-six—would have been a natural cause for slowing down. Yet according to Mary Catherine McAllister, he married his third wife, Sarah Bella Dunlop of Chambersburg, on May 6, 1826.

Around 1827, the construction of the Main Line of the Pennsylvania Canal connecting Philadelphia to Pittsburgh began, a major engineering feat of its day. Archibald's son John played a role in its construction. The canal caused Archibald considerable consternation, because it cut his property in two. The government had set a precedent to provide compensation for damages sustained to property owners by the construction of public works, and Archibald apparently was aware that he was eligible to receive such monies, for on November 21, 1826, he wrote to canal commissioner Charles Mowry for an advance on his compensation in the form of a loan "not to exceed $400." This letter is an early indication of personal financial difficulties for Archibald. But the amount of the official award had yet to be determined, and Mowry's reply was a courteous but firm no.

Running north and south parallel to the river, and three to four hundred feet from it, the route of the canal effectively bisected Archibald's property. It also crossed his millrace, coming between his millpond and sawmill, gristmill, and distillery. To answer this problem, the Canal Company proposed the construction of a culvert to run the millrace under the canal. But Archibald argued that a culvert would not provide the water velocity his businesses needed, causing him great loss. In a series of letters to the Canal Board, he proposed that the ideal solution for all concerned was to place the canal along the bank of the river. His words were not heeded. Charles Mowry, after examining Archibald's property, wrote a scathing letter to the Canal

Board against Archibald's claims. This problem and the correspondence continued for years.

A spate of advertisements placed by Archibald beginning in 1828 suggest some dramatic changes in his life. An ad of January 17, 1828, reads:

FORT HUNTER FARM AND TAVERN, TO BE RENTED, FOR one or more years, from the FIRST OF APRIL NEXT, situated on the Susquehanna six miles above Harrisburg. There is about 130 acres, under cultivation 35 of which is meadow, the [illegible] buildings such as barn, hay houses, cider house, a large stone stable in complete order for the Tavern, stone spring house smokehouse &c.—Also a large distillery, worked by steam, with all the apparatus in good order; a merchant mill within 50 yards of the still house, for terms apply to the subscriber on the premises.
Archibald McAllister. Fort Hunter, Jan 10

Two ominous advertisements appeared in the *Pennsylvania Reporter and Daily Herald* in 1828. On December 9, 1828, Archibald advertised, "For Sale, I wish to dispose of all my colored people at private sale." The advertisement goes on to describe one slave and three indentured servants, three females and one male, and their abilities. It ran several times into February. On December 24, he placed a second advertisement that read, "RAN AWAY from the subscriber at Fort Hunter, six miles above Harrisburg on the 19th instant, a female slave, named Sall Crage, aged about 60. I hereby forewarn all persons from harboring her, and will pay $2 to any person who will deliver her to me at Fort Hunter." Clearly Sall Crage, or Sal Craig, was frightened of being sold to a new owner. She had been with Archibald since she was fourteen, as shown earlier in the Register of Black Slaves and Ser-

g, and how often I was
l company, and go to
n sorrow and silence—
you'll see me some of
r being, and wel too—
mber that I applied to
GREEN, who resides in
has made me well. This
subject of our conver-
l talents have enabled
dy, which posesses the
ing this affliction.
o be put into the ears,
ardly, and its principle
en the whole nervous

t most cases of loss of
weakness of the nerves
a loss of eyesight, is ow-
the nerves of the eyes.

he whole nervous sys-
s become strengthened
sequently, recover their
and then the people get
r eye-sight again."
the Doctor's principle,
bold to say, that a more
ver, and as I, (you know)
myself, though dont prac-
be allowed to have some

ighbors asked my advice,
r wrote and had the rem-
ail   The benefit thereof
d all expense was only
rs, according to their cir-

sent on, and in return
much desired, and as a
they could pursue their

THE TIME OF COLORED PEOPLE

FOR SALE.

I wish to dispose of all my colored people
at private sale:—One female slave, aged about
sixty one years, strong and active of her age,
she is an excellent washer, baker and cook,
and understands the management of a dairy,
and soap boiling.

ALSO, a female aged about twenty years,
has eight years to serve; she understands all
kind of house work, and is stout and healthy.

ALSO, a male aged about twenty four years,
has four years to serve, remarkably stout and
healthy, and understands all kinds of farming
whatever.

ALSO, a female aged twenty two years, has
six years to serve, stout and healty, understands all kind of house work, a good cook
and ironer; in short, she understands every
kind of work that belongs to a respectable
family.

Archibald M'Allister.
December 9.

ADVERTISEMENT.

RAN AWAY from the subscriber at
Fort Hunter, six miles above Harrisburg
on the 19th instant, a female slave, named *Sall Crage,* aged abut 60.   I hereby
forewarn all persons from harboring her,
and will pay $2 to any person who will
deliver her to me at Fort Hunter.

Archibald M'Allister.
December 24, 1828.   3t.

NOTICE.

*These advertisements ran in newspapers in
1828.*

vants in 1780, and would have been
sixty-two in 1828. The original advertisement described her as "strong and active
of her age, she is an excellent washer,
baker and cook, and understands the
management of a dairy and soap boiling." Sall appears by this description to
have been the principal house servant.
Her descendants are buried at the black
cemetery at Fort Hunter under the tomb-
stone of J. Craig.

This information gives Fort Hunter
the unfortunate distinction of being one
of the last slave-owning properties in
Dauphin County. The fact that Archibald
would dispose of such a valuable worker
and member of the family indicates that
his fortunes had by now shifted. A mortgage on his property in 1828 is further
evidence of financial difficulties.

In an era of unregulated banking
and economic optimism, bankers and
individuals were loaning money freely.

Farmers, flush with money, began pro-
ducing more than the economy could
use, and an agricultural depression en-
sued. Undoubtedly financial optimism
and the vagaries of the national economy had led to the hardship Archibald
now was facing.

On September 21, 1830, he wrote a
pleading letter to the Canal Board that
ends by saying:

*I am too old to support myself by the labour of
my hand—I am now within a few months of
75—when in the revolutionary war, living for
months together with nothing but a few [illegi-
ble] under [illegible], and a single blanket over
me, and often without a cent. I little thought of
having my property taken without my consent,
and without compensation—put yourself in my
situation and I will submit to your decision—
please to excuse this scraw, I write in a great
deal of pain, both in mind and body.*
Archibald McAllister.

On March 20, 1830, the following
ad appeared in *The Republican and Anti-
Masonic Inquirer.* Undoubtedly written
by Archibald, it gives detailed insights
into the improvements on the property
at the time.

*A Valuable Farm. The Subscriber wishes to dis-
pose of the FORT HUNTER ESTATE, six miles
above Harrisburg, on the Susquehanna, CON-
TAINING 277 ACRES, 150 of which is under
cultivation, the remainder well timbered. The
improvements are a Merchant Mill, Plaster
Mill, and Saw Mill, and a large Distillery, a
cooper's Shop, a smith's shop, with Tenant
Houses, Spring houses, Garden and stable to
each—also, a tenant house, Garden and Stable
for the saw miller and Grist Miller, with all
necessary outhouses for the Farm, such as
spring house, smoke house, ice house, apple
kiln for drying apples, &c. Also a Press-House
upon a large scale, entirely enclosed, Barn, &c.
The Dwelling House is large and well adapted*

14

for a Public House—it has been kept as one for 44 years past—the Orchard, and Cider House are superior to any thing of the kind in the state. Any person inclining to purchase, can view the premises at any time. A further description is thought unnecessary, as the place is well known through the greater part of the state. If not sold before the first of April next, it will be sold on that day at public sale, and an indisputable title given for the premises by Arch'd McAllister. Fort Hunter, Jan. 23, 1830. The Editors of the Lancaster Herald and United States Gazette, Philadelphia, will give the above a few insertions.

Upon Archibald's death on January 12, 1831, at age seventy-five, he was buried with typical, if slightly old-fashioned, head- and footstones next to his second wife, Elizabeth, in the family plot on the property beyond the Pennsylvania Canal, which was not yet open. The damage claim to the Canal Company was still unsettled at the time of his death. His debts became public record. An inventory of the estate, filed on March 2, 1831, lists seven pages of household furnishings, as well as three hogsheads of apple whiskey valued at $75, "two stills and appertanances" at $60, and the "unexpired time of [two indentured] Coulard servants," Lands at $35 and Eliza at $90. His personal property inventory was valued at approximately $1,229.50. However, his debts at the time of his death totaled $5,478.65. To satisfy these debts, on January 26, 1833, the Fort Hunter property was sold at public auction by the sheriff of Dauphin County. Archibald's son John managed to bring together a consortium to purchase the property for $7,800.

Details about John's life are somewhat sporadic. He was tall, at six feet, three and a half inches, and he had a natural ability with horses, which would prove beneficial in a country setting such

as Fort Hunter. On October 27, 1812, he married Frances Harris Hanna (1791–1867), another in the McAllister family's series of socially, as well as presumably financially, advantageous marriages. Frances was the daughter of John Andre Hanna of Flemington, New Jersey, and Mary Reed Harris, the daughter of Harrisburg founder John Harris. Thus any offspring of this marriage would have the locally noble connection of being great-grandchildren of the founder of Harrisburg. John and Frances had twelve children, eight of whom lived to maturity.

In 1812, at age twenty-two, John assisted in the moving of the state government from Lancaster to Harrisburg. Francis R. Shunk, a clerk in the surveyor general's office, was assigned to accompany the public records of that department during the transfer. Mary Catherine McAllister recorded that these documents were transported to Harrisburg by a six-horse team, driven by

John Carson McAllister. COURTESY DOROTHY MACALLISTER BOYLES FAMILY

"John C. McAllister, of Fort Hunter, [while] Mr. Shunk rode all the way from Lancaster to Harrisburg on the off horse, and thus made his entrance into the new Capitol of the State, of which he was afterwards to become Governor." This is said to have been the first meeting of John McAllister and Francis Shunk, and the beginning of a lifelong friendship. Shunk's person and influence were to reappear throughout John's life.

A ledger and daybook inscribed "John C. McAllister, Fort Hunter, November 15th 1815" firmly places twenty-five-year-old John at Fort Hunter and suggests his work there as a manager. About this time, an addition was placed on the old Tavern House, perhaps to house John and his growing family.

John served as the first captain of the Dauphin County Cavalry, receiving his commission on July 30, 1824. With his troop, Captain McAllister acted as an escort to Pennsylvania governor John A. Shulze when he met Lafayette at Morrisville, Pennsylvania, on September 27, 1824, during Lafayette's visit to the United States. This mission of honor suggests responsible character as well as political connections.

Perhaps the most significant phase of John McAllister's life began in the last half of the 1820s, when he participated in the building of the most ambitious and revolutionary public works program of the day. The building of the Pennsylvania Canal challenged engineering minds and stimulated economic growth through the transportation of raw materials and finished goods. New towns sprouted up along its lines, and the expansion of the country was encouraged by the creation of a direct route from the old cities of the East Coast to the unsettled West. John played several roles in this pivotal project, including superin-

tendent, supervisor, acting commissioner of the Eastern Division of the Pennsylvania Canal for eighteen years, and superintendent of both the Wiconisco Canal and the Gettysburg Railroad.

The Pennsylvania Canal became the preferred and popular mode of travel east and west. American author Harriet Beecher Stowe traveled this route in 1841, and English author Charles Dickens made the same trip in 1842. These famous people and many more passed through Fort Hunter and enjoyed the same majestic view of the mountains and river that exists today. Dickens described the Fort Hunter area thus:

As night came on, and we drew in sight of the first range of hills, which are the outposts of the Allegheny Mountains, the scenery, which has been uninteresting hitherto, became more bold and striking. The wet ground reeked and smoked after the heavy fall of rain; and the croaking of the frogs (whose noise in these parts is almost incredible) sounded as though a million of fairy teams with bells were traveling through the air and keeping pace with us.

John's earliest official business on record with the Pennsylvania Canal involves his collection of damages on August 22, 1828. A note in the awarding of the compensation states that John Carson McAllister be "paid fifty dollars for the destruction of his hay crop, caused by the location and construction of the said canal through his father's land (he being a renter) and other damages suffered by the progress of the work through the farm."

The death of John McAllister's father, Archibald, in 1831, during the building of the canal, certainly complicated his life. John had to mourn the passing of his father, help in the settling of his per-

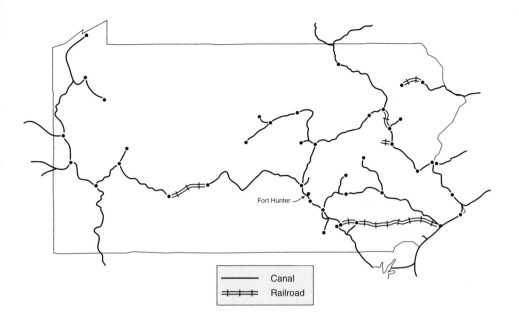

Map Legend:
- Canal
- +++ Railroad

Fort Hunter

Begun in 1828, the Main Line of the Pennsylvania Canal began in Philadelphia and extended west to Pittsburgh. By crossing the Allegheny Mountains, it opened the western part of the country to development.

sonal estate, extricate Archibald's real estate from a sheriff's sale, and maintain his involvement with his own large family, as well as various business interests. John had been raising his family at Fort Hunter, according to the census of 1830, and now the threat of the sale of the property to satisfy a mortgage loomed. A cryptic excerpt from a letter from his oldest brother, George, in Savannah, to John on November 30, 1832, suggests some of the complications involved in settling their father's estate:

Dear [John] Carson, . . . I regret the place has been sold, as I had it in contemplation to be present when sold, but a variety of circumstances beyond my control has presented. If the place is resold, as you intend it shall be, and can be put off until the 15th of December or longer, if practicable, I will then come on and see what can be done for the [illegible] of the Estate. The Sheriff has much in his power and

if [illegible] can indulge us, and [illegible] for this accommodation, you can assure him it will then be sold with the consent of all concerned.

In January 1833, a consortium made up of John Carson McAllister and two local wealthy landowners and speculators bought the property at public auction. On September 4, 1834, John, acting as administrator of his father's estate, received from the commonwealth $7,337 for damages caused by the construction of the Pennsylvania Canal. The case had moved on to the Supreme Court of Pennsylvania, and Archibald, though deceased almost four years and his property auctioned at a sheriff's sale, had finally won.

John's friend Francis Shunk purchased Harris's interest in the Fort Hunter property, and finally, on October 20, 1842, Shunk sold his interest to John Carson for $8,600. This included four

Railroads quickly replaced the canal. In 1849, this bridge was built south of Fort Hunter to carry the railroad over the Susquehanna River and west.

tracts of land totaling about 408 acres. Thus John had successfully retained the family estate, and the McAllister family was able to maintain their stronghold at the foot of Fishing Creek Valley.

Entries in John's daily account books from 1841 through 1850 present a relatively clear picture of the diversified and bustling daily comings and goings at Fort Hunter during that decade. By the 1840s, a great variety of merchandise was available for sale through what appears to be a dry-goods store operated by John. Such staples as flour, potatoes, lard, vinegar, cornmeal, molasses, sugar, and salt were sold. Meats included sausage, veal, pork, beef, shad, and—unexpectedly, because of the distance from the coast—herring and mackerel. Log rafts were purchased, and large amounts of lumber were sold from the sawmill, notably to the Pennsylvania Canal, later the Canal and Railroad Company. The books also note wheat, rye, oats, and flour from the gristmill, and include records of cows and calving, along with the arrival dates and accounts of boarders. The sales of whiskey and cider are listed, as well as such finished goods as a coffee boiler, yards of muslin, shoes, half

soles, candles, an apron, a shawl, shirts, and stockings.

In January 1845, Francis Rawn Shunk was elected governor of the state of Pennsylvania. On March 13, 1848, Governor Shunk gave John McAllister, age fifty-seven, a political commission as flour inspector of the city and county of Philadelphia—a job, no doubt, resulting from his friendship with the governor, but also perhaps due to his experience at the gristmill at Fort Hunter. In July that same year, however, Shunk was forced to resign because of illness. He died shortly thereafter.

During 1847 to 1849, yet another engineering feat was being accomplished in John's front yard: The Pennsylvania Railroad was constructing the first railroad bridge across the river just south of Fort Hunter at Rockville. Instead of the line proceeding up to Clark's Ferry to cross the Susquehanna, as the canal had run, the railroad engineers chose this more southern route. This first bridge, constructed of wood on stone piers and 3,670 feet long, carried a single track and was a dramatic accomplishment at the time.

Few records exist regarding John after this time. Though he was too old to fight in the Civil War, his three older sons, aged thirty-nine, forty-five, and forty-seven in 1860, all served their country and survived. (His two younger boys had already died in 1858 and 1859.)

On December 16, 1866, at age seventy-six, John Carson McAllister died. He was buried in the family plot on the Fort Hunter property, and his grave is marked with a simple, sturdy engraved stone. He left a basic will giving everything to his "well beloved and faithful wife Frances McAllister." Upon Frances's death on November 12, 1867, John's estate was divided equally among his children. Because some of his children were

The oldest known photograph of the Fort Hunter Mansion, this picture was taken in 1868 when John McAllister's daughters took in summer boarders.

now living out of state, they decided to sell the property. The gristmill, along with twenty-three acres, was divided off and sold to Abraham Ream on March 19, 1868, for $7,000.

In 1870, the rest of the property was put up for sale. One of the original posters advertising the sale of the property still exists at Fort Hunter. The property remains today as described in the poster. While surrounding acreage was added and subtracted over the next century, the land and the structures mentioned continued to form the nucleus of the estate. The boundaries of the railroad, canal, Fishing Creek, and the river have remained constant up to the present.

These posters were tacked up on trees to announce the sale of the Fort Hunter property in 1870.

FOR SALE

FORT HUNTER

And the adjacent un-sold real estate of CAPTAIN JOHN C. M'ALLISTER, deceased, is beautifully located on the river about six miles above Harrisburg. In all about 200 Acres, which will be sold either in whole or in parts, to suit purchasers.

IF NOT sold at Private Sale, it will be sold at Public Sale at the COURT HOUSE, in Harrisburg, on

SATURDAY, JULY 30, 1870,

next, at one o'clock P. M.

NO. 1. All that valuable piece of land at the Junction of Fishing Creek and the Susquehanna river, containing five acres and a-half, having thereon a large **TWO-STORY STONE MANSION**

HOUSE.

A Stone Bank Barn, and other buildings, an orchard, &c , suitable for a country seat or for a First-class Hotel.

NO. 2. All that valuable piece of land adjoining No 1, fronting on the river and extending back to the Pennsylvania Canal, containing 20 Acres, suitable for building lots, No. 2 can be sold with No 1 if desirable.

NO. 3. All that valuable piece of land adjoining Nos. 1 and 2, and the Mill Property with 5 Acres and 53 perches, West of the Pennsylvania Canal, and 30 Acres between the Canal and the Schuylkill and Susquehanna Railroad, being in all 35 Acres and 53 perches, thereon erected a STONE and PLASTERED HOUSE, and a large STONE STABLE; it has also a fine spring and spring-house; the premises being suitable for a truck farm. *Saw Mill & c &c &c*

NO. 4. All that valuable piece of land west of Fishing Creek, adjoining lands of Dr. Louis Heck, with wharfage on the Canal and on the Railroad, containing 10 Acres.

NO. 5. All that valuable piece of land west of the Fishing Creek road, adjoining lands of Dr. Louis Heck and James Reed, containing 26 Acres and 68 perches, nearly all cleared and under good fences.

NO. 6. All that valuable PLANTATION adjoining the Susquehanna railroad, Fishing Creek and the lands of James Reed and No. 5, containing 95 Acres, all in cultivation and under good fences.

A plot of the land can be seen at the office of Hamilton Alricks, No. 308 Market Street, Harrisburg. Terms: Twenty per cent, (or security for payment of same within thirty days to be given) when the property is sold; thirty per cent more on the 1st day of October next, when deed will be made (at the cost of the purchaser) and possession given, and the other half in one year, to be secured by bond and mortgage.

ARCHIBALD M'ALLISTER,
RICHARD M'ALLISTER,

Executors of John C. M'Allister, deceased.

The Pleasures of Victorian Country Life, 1870-1933

Daniel Dick Boas purchased the venerable Fort Hunter property in 1870. Already a successful businessman, Daniel's earlier life reads like a Horatio Alger story.

He was born in Harrisburg on February 19, 1816, four and a half months after the death of his father, Jacob Boas. Soon after Daniel's birth, his mother, Sarah Dick Boas, and her five sons moved to Reading, Pennsylvania, to live with Sarah's family. At the appropriate time in his life, he was apprenticed to learn a trade. After this time, he took a position in the Harrisburg post office.

On November 23, 1840, he married Margaret Bates, a native of Ireland and a member of the Church of England. She became a lifelong member of St. Stephen's Episcopal Church and later a founder of the Home for the Friendless, today known as Homeland.

Daniel went into business with Oliver P. Bellman, who was involved in the shoe trade. The partners abandoned the shoe business in 1842 to begin a lumberyard in the Shipoke neighbor-hood in south Harrisburg. Later he bought his partner out. In 1867, Daniel expanded his business with a saw and planing mill. Handling such items as window sashes and shutters, bar and store fixtures, and doors, his business thrived. At the time, Harrisburg was rapidly expanding as a rail-road hub with a

Daniel Dick and Margaret Bates Boas were leading citizens of Harrisburg.

great need for housing. Perceiving that wave, and already turning a profit on the materials used to build homes, Daniel also saw the longer-term benefits of owning houses himself and began building and owning rental properties. He collected rent on about sixty houses on streets including 2nd, 3rd, 4th, 6th, 7th, Boas, Reily, Briggs, Cameron, Paxton, Hummel, Logan, Boyd, Williams, Market, and Vine.

In spite of his business successes, his primary residence was a compact and rather dowdy home that he built in 1843 on fashionable North Front Street, across Cranberry Street from St. Stephen's Episcopal Church in downtown Harrisburg. He was a member of St. Stephen's and served as a warden and the treasurer for the parish for many years.

His family had grown to five children. His first child, Sarah Tyler, was born on March 2, 1842. She was followed by William Stuart on July 21, 1843, Jane (Jennie) Eliza in 1848, and Henry (Harry) Dick Boas, on October 11, 1851. Daniel and Margaret's last child, named Helen Margaret, was born ten years later, on November 8, 1861. She would later become the last mistress of the Fort Hunter Mansion.

Daniel was involved in many community activities. He was a firm believer in the relatively new concept of a free education for children. As such, he served on the School Board of Harrisburg for many years and was president of that body for eighteen years. He is credited with encouraging the construction of many of the school buildings at the time, and Boas School was named after him, as was Boas Street.

In 1870, Daniel's second son, Henry, came to work for him at the lumbermill. It was also in that year that the Fort Hunter property came up for sale. When Daniel learned of the impending sale, his

This was the conservative Front Street home of the Boas family in Harrisburg.

speculative as well as agricultural interests led him to investigate. What he found was a group of antiquated yet sturdy stone buildings on fertile, scenic, and well-situated land that was very conveniently located near the city. On September 22, 1870, Daniel bought the Fort Hunter property at public auction for $20,500. The 182 acres he purchased straddled Fishing Creek in both Susquehanna and Middle Paxton Townships. The deed states that the first tract contained "the Fort Hunter Mansion" and specifically excludes the McAllister family cemetery.

In purchasing Fort Hunter, Daniel Dick Boas became one of a growing breed of financially comfortable individuals of the Gilded Age who set their sights on taking the mystery out of farming by introducing science into the agricultural equation. Scientific farming had been in existence, but in the last half of the nineteenth century, it surged forward with renewed enthusiasm and money. Wealth earned from other businesses allowed men of means the time and money to indulge in farming experiments. These businessmen became known as "gentleman farmers."

Scientific farming proved a test for the intellect. The central Pennsylvania region was nationally reputed as a very fertile area, yet farming was predomi-

Top right: This early view of the Fort Hunter Barn, built in 1876, shows the three spire-like ventilators on the roof.
Bottom right: The Mansion House received an Italianate front porch, heavy hoods over the windows, and a somber paint scheme.
Below: The old Tavern House had been renovated into a home for the dairy crew.

nantly done in old-fashioned ways, even when the reasons for these ways had vanished with the years. Information was simply handed down from father to son by word of mouth. Scientific farming set about testing these traditions and sometimes changing them.

Economies of time and space were the easiest to challenge and were the most interesting to these new farmers. The thought was that if buildings were arranged in the proper order, work could be performed more efficiently, therefore increasing the efficiency of the entire farm and creating greater return on the energy expended. In essence, the businessmen introduced assembly line manufacturing processes to farming. Often these theories were illustrated with idealized drawings of attractive farms laid out according to the philosophy, and with the buildings made up of matching architectural elements. But in reality, rare was the farm that was purchased, planned, and built all at one time. More

likely, the farm had grown and changed over the years. The gentleman farmer developed a great appreciation for the overall visual integrity and neatness of his idealized farm. The farmer would conclude that a neat and organized farm would reflect well upon its owners, too, and it perpetuated other moral theories of neatness, which were pervading a society short on history and, at the time, nervous about stability.

Daniel Dick Boas subscribed wholeheartedly to this theory at Fort Hunter. That he owned a planing mill, which could provide supplies for alterations at cost, undoubtedly helped in his decision to give all of the structures a face-lift. Up-to-date buildings would certainly reflect upon Daniel in the community, because thousands of travelers passed the property yearly. Not only would the renovations make an impact on people in the community, but they would also serve as an advertisement for his lumber products.

The specific order in which the remodeling took place is unknown. What is clear is that virtually every structure on the property was renovated within a relatively short span of time during the 1870s. The most significant alteration was the demolition of an unrecorded barn on the east side of the River Road, as Front Street was then called, and the construction of the large barn that stands today. Built to house a budding dairy operation, it was constructed in the traditional Pennsylvania German bank barn form but with elaborate decorative details.

All of the other buildings and outbuildings on the property were updated with exaggerated trim and given a cohesive paint scheme. Fashionable deep red sashes contrasted subtly with dark chocolate brown trim on all the structures. These colors cleverly brought out the natural hues of the local stone. The overall effect on all the buildings was stylish, subtle, crisp, clean, and beautifully wedded to the surrounding landscape.

Aside from the improvements to his real estate, Daniel was actively involved behind the scenes in politics, and in 1876 he was a Democratic presidential elector. It was said that "he declined, or rather refused to be a candidate for office, oftener than any man so prominent in politics as he, because, [he preferred] to fight in the ranks of his party, to any position as leader."

Daniel's enjoyment of the renovations to his farm was short lived. On the evening of May 9, 1878, while returning from a visit to his farm at Fort Hunter with County Commissioner S. Boyd Martin, Daniel was killed in a carriage accident.

As was the custom of the time, formal mourning rituals were quickly set in motion. Black clothes were ordered, stationery and calling cards with wide bor-

ders of black ink signifying deep mourning were printed, a wreath ornamented with a black ribbon was affixed to the front door, and mirrors were draped with cloth inside the 213 North Front Street house.

Befitting a man of his stature, Daniel's body was buried in a family plot in the Harrisburg Cemetery high on a hill overlooking the city. Signifying a shift from family plots in the country or churchyard cemeteries in the city, which were becoming overly crowded and unsanitary, the suburban "cemetery park" was becoming increasingly popular. It provided bucolic surroundings, with romantically designed curving paths and drives, and landscaping of evergreens and weeping trees full of symbolism. In such an environment, it was considered appropriate for family members to pack a picnic and walk to the family member's grave to enjoy a repast, with the knowledge that the entire family was, indeed, together.

Daniel Dick Boas was sixty-two years old on his death. His youngest child, Helen Margaret, was seventeen, and his wife, Margaret Bates, was fifty-nine. He

This unlabeled photograph in the Fort Hunter collection shows the custom of family members picnicking in a cemetery. Note the dog carrying the picnic basket.

Helen Boas as a child.

with pragmatism, a trait still highly valued in the traditional Harrisburg community. As the youngest daughter of older, monied parents, Helen was probably indulged, and she was said to be an unusually attractive child. By the time of her birth, her family was well established in Harrisburg society, with all of its accoutrements, formalities, and responsibilities. As members of the Front Street circle, they were invited to all of the parties and events, and they hobnobbed with the other well-to-do people of the city. Calling cards with "Miss Boas" and "Helen M. Boas" were printed for the formal social obligations befitting a young woman of her stature.

Summers at Fort Hunter were a highlight of her early life. Her sketchbooks record lovely drawings of her environment. Young Helen drew such views as the old stone arch bridge over Fishing Creek, a fishing rod and creel leaning against a plank bottom chair, and the front facade of the Mansion House.

Helen was almost nine years old when her father purchased the property. It must have seemed like a magical spot. The views of the Susquehanna and the fishing holes of Fishing Creek would have provided endless hours of entertainment. While traffic on the River Road was less steady than that in the city, steam locomotives charged through

died without a will. Because of the complexity of the estate and the fact that one of the children, Helen, was still a minor, the assets remained intact and were administered for years as an estate, with both Margaret and her oldest son, William, as executors. This tied the family's financial interests together for their lifetimes, and it also reflected the prevailing attitude of the time—that women were incapable of handling money and required a man's supervision.

The history of Fort Hunter during the years immediately following the death of Daniel Dick Boas remains unclear. The dairy farm probably remained active and was run by Daniel's estate. The Mansion had never been the primary residence of the Boas family and so perhaps remained a country home for the heirs and their families. But upon the marriage of Helen Margaret Boas in 1887, the Mansion came into use as a year-round residence once again.

Born into a privileged life, Helen enjoyed the benefits of wealth combined

This sketch of the bridge over Fishing Creek at Fort Hunter was drawn by Helen Boas in 1876.

Fort Hunter, and canal boats passed by at their usual leisurely pace. All provided a changing panorama of interesting people for young Helen. In the country, she became comfortable on a horse. She wore a heavy blue wool suit with asymmetrically cut skirt to cover her legs while sitting sidesaddle, and a beaver-skin top hat.

The sudden death of her father in 1878, when she was seventeen, was a shock to the sheltered Helen. The loss of a doting parent would turn the world of any teenager upside down. But in spite of the disruption caused by her father's death, Helen was sent to the Chestnut Street Female Seminary in Philadelphia. She graduated on June 15, 1880.

In keeping with American traditions of the time and of young women of her class, Helen went on a grand tour of Europe with her mother, leaving in May 1881 and returning five months later. While America was experiencing unbounded economic success, the arts were still considered to be in their infancy—rough by European and, hence, world standards. To achieve the goal of a cultured daughter, the grand tour became *de rigueur* for girls of prominent families. Under her mother's watchful eye, Helen

Helen Boas was an accomplished equestrian.

enjoyed visits to England, Ireland, Scotland, Holland, Belgium, France, Germany, and Switzerland.

On November 3, 1887, after a lengthy courtship, Helen Boas married John Whitehill Reily. The wedding was of such significance as to warrant the full center column of the front page of the Harrisburg *Evening Star* on November 4, 1887.

John Reily was also from an established Harrisburg family. He was born September 26, 1860, at 6 South Market Square, the son of Dr. John Whitehill and Katherine E. (Dull) Reily. His father died on March 20 of the same year, before John was born. John's mother later married Dr. William H. Harris, a descendant of the founder of Harrisburg, who died in 1884. No letters from Dr. Harris to John survive, suggesting that his involvement in John's life was limited.

John Whitehill Reily as a young man.

Charles L. Bailey, owner
of the Chesapeake Nail
Works and president of
the Central Iron Works,
and Gilbert M. McCauley,
treasurer and manager of
the Central Iron Works,
were these guardians. Bailey was very busy with
the operations of his
business, so it fell to
"Uncle Mac" to arrange
for the payment of bills.
Childless, he also seemed
to take a great interest in
John's general welfare
and offered much pater-
nal advice, which, for the
most part, John took. His
sister, Bessie, and half-sister, Sally, also dutifully
wrote John at school.

John then attended
the prestigious Phillips
Academy at Andover, Massachusetts, and
graduated on June 18, 1879. At the time
of his graduation, a young man of John's
means and education had two options.
If he wished to enter into a profession
such as law, banking, or medicine, he
might attend college. If he preferred to
enter the business world, he would get a
job in that business and learn it from
within. There was some talk of Prince-
ton, but John ultimately decided on the
business world.

August 1879 found John, now referred to in some letters as Jack, working
in the Harrisburg National Bank for his
uncle George Reily, who was president of
the bank. But by February 1880, through
arrangements made by his uncles Mac

John had an older sister, Rebecca Elizabeth (Bessie), and a half-sister, Sara E.
Harris (Sally).

John was first taught in the private
school of Miss Woodward of Harrisburg,
which promoted itself as "the best and
most popular private school" in the city.
He then moved on to the Harrisburg
Academy, under the auspices of a Profes-
sor Seilor. From 1873 to 1876, he attended the McClellan Institute at West
Chester. Letters to John from this period
have Uncle Gilbert M. "Mac" McCauley
sending him $5 now and then for his
passage home for holidays. Correspondence with John makes it clear that his
two uncles, who were married to John's
mother's sisters, served as his guardians.

and Charlie, he began his business career with the Montgomery Iron Company at their mills in Port Kennedy, Pennsylvania. He was a clerk and assistant manager there until 1881, at which point he was appointed superintendent of the Union Forge in Lebanon County, where he remained until 1883.

John's ambitions, however, were greater than working for someone else. In January 1882, he began discussing with his uncle Mac the possibility of going into business for himself. John was coming of age and would soon be responsible for the modest estate set up for him upon his father's death. Uncle Mac was aware of John's personal finances and determined that a partnership would be necessary. He began arranging such a partnership with the Seidel brothers in the Harrisburg area. Apparently John approved of his uncle's plan, for on May 20, 1882, at age twenty-two, he entered into a copartnership with them, called Reily, Seidel & Co., to build and operate a scrap forge.

The agreement was framed to last for five years, after which the mortgage and bond that the Seidels carried for half of the business would be paid off. Land was purchased to erect the forge just north of the city of Harrisburg, along the railroad lines. It was located just south of Linglestown Road, west of the Pennsylvania Canal, and east of the Pennsylvania Railroad. For an unknown reason, it was named Lucknow Forge. Perhaps John was looking for luck, now.

It was also around this time that John began courting Helen Boas, known to her friends as "Boasy." In keeping with the rules of propriety of the time, it was a lengthy courtship, fraught with elaborate and intricate social etiquette. Gentle ribbing in a letter from a friend suggests a serious interest in Helen as early as August 20, 1882: "So this time its Miss Boas on the string—I have a mighty hard time keeping track of you. Well, Fort Hunter would be a nice place to live. So near the Forge 'you know.'"

Helen and John had known each other for a long time, and eventually they were deemed an appropriate match. After a five-year courtship, they were married on November 3, 1887. John was twenty-seven, and Helen would turn twenty-seven in a matter of days. Shortly before that time, John became the sole owner of Lucknow Forge.

They were immediately offered the use of the Fort Hunter Mansion as their home. It was a very large house for just the two of them. Photographs of the interiors taken within a year of their marriage show rooms demurely wallpapered and economical sticks of furniture scattered far away from each other.

Throughout their lives, the Mansion, along with Daniel Dick Boas's original

The Lucknow Forge is depicted on the company stationery.

In the Reilys' early married years, the parlor of the Mansion looked bare.

purchase of 182 acres, would remain tied to the Boas estate, of which Helen was one of six beneficiaries. Regardless, John and Helen Reily began an aggressive campaign of securing surrounding acreage. As early as 1888, regular payments of $300 were being made for the approximately two-hundred-acre Chuckey Hill Property, now the Fort Hunter Conservancy. Eventually the Reilys owned a staggering fourteen hundred acres at Fort Hunter. John Reily's obituary said he "maintained a mode of life similar to that maintained by landed Englishmen." On the practical side, the timber on these large landholdings proved beneficial to the forge, which re-

quired great quantities of charcoal, and the open spaces served the Fort Hunter Dairy for grazing. The estate was of such magnitude as to warrant a separate summer cabin for entertaining, called Guadaloupe, which was about a mile away from the Mansion.

The Reilys' business and financial lives were diverse. John's Lucknow Forge was the main source of their income. It used an iron-making process from scraps to produce iron "blooms"—ingots similar to pig-iron—suitable for other factories to melt down and remake into such things as sheet iron, wire, and boiler plates. John operated Lucknow Forge for thirty-six years. On February 1, 1926, he sold the property for $55,000 to the Pennsylvania Railroad, which continued to run it as a plant for the reclaiming of scrap iron and steel for the entire railroad system.

While operating the forge, John Reily also assumed complete charge of the Boas dairy farm at Fort Hunter. According to his biography, the farm was ninety acres at the beginning of his manage-

Above: The cabin called Guadaloupe was the site of many informal parties. Left: The Guadaloupe interior was eclectically furnished.

This booklet touted the benefits of the Fort Hunter Dairy.

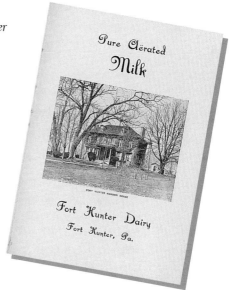

ment and, by 1907, had grown to fourteen hundred acres. According to a description of the Fort Hunter Dairy in 1907, John "has three hundred cow, two hundred of which are milk cows, and the milk from these is retailed in the city of Harrisburg, carried to his various customers in wagons. He has eighty head of horses and mules, and gives employment to sixty-five hands." An undated eleven-page booklet touts the product from Fort Hunter as "Pure Aërated Milk." Using ten black-and-white photographs of Fort Hunter and an upbeat text, this booklet sells the reader on this healthful and sanitary product.

In addition to the forge and the dairy, the farm also contained a stone quarry that, according to the 1930 *Encyclopedia of Pennsylvania Biography,* "supplie[d] a fine quality of building stone, crushed stone and gravel, and was long a source of revenue to Mr. Reily, until he leased the property to the Rockville Quarry Company." This quarry also supplied gravel for the Fort Hunter Road Commission.

Yet another form of income came from the Daniel Dick Boas Estate. An accounting sheet titled "Rents—D. D. Boas Estate" of September 1899, lists rental income from fifty-nine houses in downtown and midtown Harrisburg. It is clear that Helen and John Reily had varied and diverse forms of income throughout their lifetimes.

The roles of employer and major landholder during these times brought with them multiple obligations. Many hardworking people were dependent upon any business decisions made by the Reilys. In an era before unemploy-

ment compensation or other social programs, employees and tenants of the Reilys often had to rely upon them in times of family sickness or emergency. In addition to their employer roles, John and Helen often had to serve as arbiters, medical providers, moneylenders, or evictors. The seasonal aspect of some of their businesses also greatly affected their workers. In these areas, being levelheaded, fair, and tough was imperative.

A quarry was also located on the Fort Hunter property.

As the Reilys did not have children, they used the third floor and the farthest reaches of the rear wing of the Mansion for storage. An overwhelming number of items belonging to the Reilys remain at Fort Hunter. Among them are Helen's diaries, clothes, and a scrapbook of news clippings. John left boxes of correspondence sent to him, including childhood letters, love letters from Helen, and business advertisements. Hundreds of photographs depict them throughout their lives—from about 1860 to 1932—and tell a great deal about them. Friends and family members figure prominently in the collection and exhibit ever-changing fashions.

Life around Fort Hunter Mansion was also captured in photos of the interior and exterior of the house in various seasons, as well as in various years, along with changes in decorating style. A new Colonial Revival style front porch, added to the Mansion around the turn of the century, appears in many photos and suggests a rekindled interest in the history of the property. John's animals are also in some of the photos, from his prize-winning farm animals to his pets, including many dogs that lived in the old icehouse and a blurry image of an orangutan that is said to have lived in the front cellar. Photos of the parrot, which resided on the west porch in good weather and was said to have had a rather foul mouth, have not yet been discovered.

Payment of regular bills to the John Wanamaker store appear in cash books of the period, probably to cover the cost of elegant clothing for Helen. Judging from the quality and quantity of women's clothing remaining in the Mansion, Helen must have been one of the most fashionably dressed women in Harrisburg. She bought clothes from Philadelphia, Pittsburgh, New York, Chicago, and even Paris. She was also known to have had unfashionable dresses updated at her home by a seamstress.

Throughout her life, Helen maintained a very active social life. She devoted a great deal of time to a variety of charities in and about the city, and she took leadership roles, often as president, in most of them. They included the Home for the Friendless (now Homeland), the YWCA (to which she gave the land for Camp Reily), the Wednesday Club (she had a notable singing voice), the Civic Club, the Needlework Guild, the Red Cross, the Maternity Hospital, and the Country Club.

The original YWCA is pictured here, with Helen Boas Reily's formal landau carriage parked in front.

John Reily at forty.

By all accounts, John was a handsome man with engaging blue eyes. A friend in Savannah wrote in 1877, "All the girls are falling in love with your picture, which I don't like at all, so I shan't show it to my sweetheart, for if she gives me up I don't know what will become of me, if she sees your picture I know full well she will." And an epitaph reads, "Mr. Reily was one of the finest looking men of Harrisburg and was beloved by many."

An outdoorsman and a sportsman, he enjoyed hunting and fishing, along with more refined, and expensive, sports such as skeet shooting, carriage driving, tobogganing, and sleigh racing. His racing sleigh and monogrammed toboggan remain in the Fort Hunter collection. His ownership of a roof seat break, or "tally-ho," drawn by teams of horses, set him apart as a whip and a sportsman. Sport vehicles of this type were used to convey large groups of people on pleasure trips about the countryside. They were rare, expensive, and required four or six matched horses and highly technical athletic skills as a "whip," or driver, which few possessed. Trips in such vehicles merited listing in the Harrisburg society pages, as well as in the pages of the newspapers of the towns visited, often listing the names of all members of the party.

A sociable man, John was one of the founders of the Inglenook Club, an early exclusive men's sporting club located on the Susquehanna River north of the Clarks Ferry Bridge. Established in 1888, it was a forerunner to the Harrisburg Country Club, of which he was also a member, and to which he sold land in 1916.

John Reily at the reins of his elegant roof seat break with a party of gentlemen on Gettysburg Battlefield.

*John Reily and
Helen Boas Reily
in their later years.*

her personal property was modest, her real estate holdings were large, and her will made specific plans to split up the land of the Fort Hunter estate, giving gifts of land to various individuals and organizations. The remaining acreage, including the buildings and noncontiguous bits of far-flung tracts, totaled about 312 acres. Of this, the original Daniel Dick Boas tracts of about 88 acres—which contained the Mansion and the farm buildings—were still tied to his residual estate. The death of Helen Boas Reily finally dissolved the D. D. Boas estate. But the dissolution led to other complications. With confusing bequests to nine scattered heirs, the future of Fort Hunter did not look hopeful.

John Reily died in his sixty-sixth year. The following was noted in a newspaper clipping in the Fort Hunter collection: "The death of Mr. Reily, which occurred September 13, 1927, after an illness of three weeks, removed from his community a citizen of superior qualities and one who had stamped his personality and influence upon those who came within their beneficent range." Helen died five years later, in 1932.

The Reilys had led lives of country elegance during the era of the Vanderbilts, Carnegies, and Morgans. Though perhaps not as wealthy as these families, their upbringing, lifestyle, and success allowed them to float regularly among them. They enjoyed carriages, fashion, society, travel, sports, public service, business, and power—all based from a beautiful, historic, and publicly visible estate.

The will left by Helen upon her death caused serious complications. Though

This photo shows the Fort Hunter Mansion around 1930.

The Making of a Museum and Park, 1933 Forward

The death of Helen Boas Reily in 1932 left the future of Fort Hunter uncertain. The country was in the Depression, the time-worn estate was in poor condition, and Helen's will had awkwardly left the property to nine nieces and nephews—none living in the Harrisburg area. Within this puzzle, one niece, Margaret Wister Meigs, immediately began pursuing a vision of her own making. Surprisingly, she saw the future of the estate as a museum of American life.

Margaret, born in 1882, was the youngest of three girls. Her older sisters were Elizabeth, known as Bessie, and Sarah. They grew up in two elegant homes, one in the city of Philadelphia, and the other in the town of Duncannon, where their father, John Wister, owned the Duncannon Iron Company. They also kept a summer home in Chester, Nova Scotia, cleverly named Wisteria. Her mother, Sarah Boas Wister, was the eldest sister of Helen Boas Reily. As a child, Margaret had enjoyed many pleasurable hours with her aunt Helen and uncle John at Fort Hunter.

The home in Duncannon allowed her father to keep an eye on the family business, while the home in Philadelphia enabled the family to maintain an active foothold in Philadelphia society.

When in Duncannon, the Wisters socialized with the Harrisburg set, and Margaret had plenty of time to get to know her aunt and uncle, as well as Fort Hunter. Margaret grew up with the benefits of being the child of the very respected owner of the primary industry in a small town, having an active social life as a member of the prominent Boas family in Harrisburg, and possessing the privileged station of a descendant of two

Margaret Wister at her sister's wedding.

33

Left: The Boas and Wister families at a picnic. Helen Boas Reily is on the left. Margaret Wister is third from the right. Below: The Wister home in Duncannon.

honorable and historic families in the large city of Philadelphia.

The home in the Germantown section of Philadelphia, known as Belfield, is rich in history as the former home of the famous Peale family of artists from 1810 to 1826. The Wister family purchased it in 1826. They enjoyed the distinction of being "from an old and distinguished Philadelphia family" known throughout the mid-Atlantic states, well traveled, and cosmopolitan. They were members of the ruling oligarchy that had held sway in Philadelphia since the eighteenth century. Not only was John a Wister, but his mother was from the prestigious Logan family. He was a Quaker and a Republican, and interestingly, Sarah Boas Wister, his wife, was an Episcopalian and a Democrat.

Margaret graduated with honors from Agnes Irwin Girls School in Philadelphia in 1900. Not an advocate of college for women, Margaret felt that women could learn enough from finishing school and an attentive mother. Yet she was taught not to be a shrinking violet, bowing behind the opinions of a husband, either. Like her mother and her aunt Helen, whom she called Auntie, Margaret was a strong woman. She had been brought up to think for herself and appreciated the importance of personal opinions and politics.

A clipping from a Harrisburg newspaper reports:

February 11, 1907. Women in Politics. Miss Margaret Wister of Belfield, Wister Station, Germantown, gave a City Party tea on Saturday afternoon. Miss Wister was assisted in receiving by a number of young women and several speakers enunciated City Party doctrine for the fair sex. Miss Wister is well known in this city [Harrisburg] and is a niece of Mrs. Henry D. Boas and Mrs. John W. Reily.

The City Party was a thinly veiled suffrage movement, offered under the guise of repairing corrupt government. They advocated the cleaning up of notoriously dirty Philadelphia politics by giving the vote to women, who then would vote crooks out of office. Margaret maintained an active voice in politics throughout her life.

Margaret enjoyed the customary "grand tour" of Europe and the innocent flirtations of men of her social strata. As early as 1898, she may have had her eye on Edward Browning Meigs. Though the world had changed, Victorian propriety

Left: The Wister home in Germantown, Philadelphia, known as Belfield. Above: Edward Browning Meigs from a portrait by Comins, 1935. COURTESY OF ANNE MEIGS-BROWN.

maintained full sway over such things in the Wister family, and among other things, Edward had to pass parental approval of his annual salary. In 1910, Edward formally proposed, and the two were wed on June 8, 1910.

Edward Meigs was a young doctor of medicine, keenly interested in research. He was the son of Dr. Arthur Vincent Meigs and Mary Roberts Browning Meigs, who maintained homes in both Philadelphia and Radnor. He became engaged to Margaret while teaching at Harvard. As native Philadelphians, Edward and Margaret shared many mutual friends and were members of the Philadelphia Assembly, an organization that had sponsored an annual society ball since the eighteenth century.

The personalities of Edward and Margaret seemed to complement each other. In her 1987 book, *The Box Closet*, their daughter, Mary, describes her perspective on the marriage as follows:

She was a woman who did not drink, smoke, wear make-up or perfume but eau de cologne (Roger and Gallet), who was simple, disciplined and chaste in her thoughts, who guarded her children ferociously from knowledge of "this wicked world," and who would have been profoundly shocked by its inner workings. A protective spell enabled both Margaret and Edward to get through life unscathed and ignorant of the most depraved kinds of wickedness; it seemed to be an essential part of their married happiness not to look into the vortex of evil, which would make them sick and dizzy. The marriage contract required the continuation of the state of innocence they shared, bound together like babes in the wood. Each was really the only good friend the other needed. In January 1910, Margaret writes Edward a little sharply, "As for being interested in your work of course I am interested in it, far more, doubtless, than you have ever considered being interested in mine." Rapping him over the knuckles as usual—but I am pleasantly surprised by her insistence on equal interest. Equally surprising is the fact that Edward un-

35

derstood what she meant. Their formula for a happy marriage was not like Horace Jencks', by which the "good woman" appears to do most of the work of sympathy and encouragement. Margaret and Edward listened to each other, after the fashion of two people whose minds are shaped so differently that they can never mesh together in total understanding. They had known this about each other from the beginning—that their minds often met in a shower of sparks or a short circuit. But they struggled with the intractable idea of marriage until death parted them.

After an exotic honeymoon abroad, the couple settled in Philadelphia. Edward was a member of the staff of the Wister Institute for the next six years. The birth of a son, Arthur Vincent, on February 3, 1912, was certainly a time of great joy. Another son, John Wister, always called Wister, was born on January 10, 1915. That same year, Edward was offered a position as a physiologist with the Bureau of Dairy Industry in the federal Department of Agriculture, and the family moved to Washington, D.C. He organized and administered the department's experimental farm, now the National Agricultural Research Station, in Beltsville, Maryland, along with a laboratory in the Department of Agriculture Building downtown. He later represented the department at the Physiological Congress in Edinburgh, Scotland, in 1923 and the World's Dairy Congress in London in 1928.

The move to Washington was drastic for both Edward and Margaret. At the same time, it had the potential to be freeing. Coming from families so immersed in Philadelphia society had its constricting effects. The life they were familiar with there had them constantly watched and judged. In the end, their reactions to the move were mixed.

"For him, Washington was freedom; for Margaret, it was exile," daughter Mary observes. His goal to "improve and cheapen the milk supply all over the world" could be focused on and achieved only in D.C., away from the social obligations of Philadelphia. Beyond his work, "Edward prefers sitting at home to doing anything." The "saucy, irrepressible Margaret" had other ideas on how to adjust to the move. First, she wasn't going to lose her personal and social connections to Philadelphia. "That was why she took the twins to Philadelphia to be born, why she took her children to visit aunts and grandmothers in Philadelphia, why the twins were put through the patriarchal mill of a Philadelphia debut, and why she tried never to miss a family wedding or funeral." Second, she would infiltrate Washington society. "In a month's time [after her arrival in Washington] she had reached two of her goals: to know the Cabinet ladies, and to be invited to the White House. She was launched in the giddy excitement of Washington society."

The surprise birth of fraternal twin daughters, Mary Roberts and Sarah Tyler, on April 27, 1917, caused great excitement throughout the entire extended family. Margaret and Edward and their babies became the focus of intense admiration. Even her sister "Bessie, who appears in Margaret's letters and diaries like a wicked older sister in a fairy story, fell for the twins."

In 1922, Margaret's mother, Sarah Tyler Boas Wister, died. Her death represented for Margaret the end of an era. Large estates in the vicinity of Belfield were being sold and chopped up into small plots for row homes. The old social clubs were on shaky ground. The manner in which people presented themselves seemed increasingly common. The Roaring Twenties were starting to growl, and Margaret wanted nothing to do with them.

The gentility and respectability that their mother represented became values that both Margaret and her sister, Sarah Logan Wister Starr, strove not only to emulate, but also to preserve. In the ever-pressing world around them in the 1920s and 1930s, these values seemed very alive, even cloistered, on the old historic properties where they had spent much of their childhood. Upon the death of their mother, Sarah was willed Belfield and determined to live there. It required gentle upgrading to meet the modern standards of comfort, yet these were added without disturbing the his-

The Meigs town house on M Street in Washington, D.C. COURTESY OF THE HISTORICAL SOCIETY OF WASHINGTON, D.C.

toric structure. These actions certainly served as a precedent for Margaret's later project at Fort Hunter.

Meanwhile, raising their family in D.C., the Meigses continued to work hard in their circles and in turn enjoyed respect in the city. In 1926, they bought the outwardly restrained but very spacious five-story, red brick town house at 1736 M Street. "The house in Washington was [her] outer garment, as much a part of [her] as a bird's feathers," Mary writes. Finally, Margaret had a beautiful and stately frame for her family and its possessions.

The home had formerly been the residence of Alice Longworth, Theodore Roosevelt's rambunctious eldest daughter, who was married to the Speaker of the House. At one particular dinner, a guest mentioned to Margaret, "The last time I had dinner in this room, the hostess, Alice, was standing on her head in that corner of the room!" Here, over the

This publicity photograph announcing the opening of the house as a museum and tearoom shows the heirs of Helen Boas Reily on the front porch of the Fort Hunter Mansion.

years, the Meigses entertained scores of Washington's movers and shakers as well.

A family of means, they enjoyed certain material assets. They employed a cook, who lived next to the kitchen in the raised basement. Two cars, a billiard table, scattered inherited investment properties, and a summer home in Woods Hole, Massachusetts, named Comtuit, all were signs of a comfortably affluent, yet pleasantly unpretentious, lifestyle.

While her husband pursued his research at work and through his memberships in several scientific clubs, Margaret became deeply involved in the community. She served on the board of trustees for the Sidwell Friends School, was a founder and twice president of the Women's National Democratic Club, and was a lifelong member of the Girls' Friendly Society of America. She served on the boards of the St. John's Orphanage and the Sulgrave Club. For many years, she held office in the Washington

Literary Society. She was also a member of the Pennsylvania Society of Colonial Dames of America and the Pennsylvania Historical Society. Margaret Wister Meigs became known as an intelligent, energetic, capable, and strong-willed woman. Her will was soon to be tested.

Mary Meigs records in *The Box Closet* that in October 1928 an X-ray examination of Edward showed "infiltration, fibrosis and one large cavity in the apex of the left lung. The appearance is that of an old tuberculous process in the right apex." This diagnosis would quietly change the family's future. At the time, the prescribed cure for tuberculoses was sanatorium rest. Edward spent most of 1929 in such an institution.

The death of Margaret's uncle John Reily in 1927 and Auntie Helen in 1932 were sentimental milestones. She had known them and Fort Hunter all her life. Photos of Helen and John often show Margaret, as a young girl, with them on picnics and outings. It is certain that she played there often. In their deaths, she could not have envisioned that she would soon be the owner of the property.

Yet 1932 found Margaret inheriting, through a complicated process, one-third of one-third of 88 acres containing the Mansion and one-ninth of an additional 224 acres. Within these worn and disjointed properties, Margaret saw the possibility of a preservation mission. At a time when cars were becoming increasingly available and roads more drivable, the American public was beginning to travel extensively, and there was a growing thirst for tourist attractions along major roads. The linear train routes no longer limited the availability to such places. Historic houses were becoming travel destinations.

While Margaret never learned to drive, the increasing popularity of the automobile, along with her interest in preserving a disappearing way of life and the recent inheritance of her share in Fort Hunter, created the seed of an idea. Her dream was to preserve Fort Hunter and exhibit a way of life that she knew had changed. With her husband's full support, she immediately began approaching her eight other cousins with the idea. A Philadelphia newspaper clipping preserved in a scrapbook announced a surprisingly quick opening:

April 20, 1933—Historic Mansion Will Be Opened by Fashionable Heirs About six miles beyond Harrisburg, on the William Penn highway, is a lovely old estate "Fort Hunter," built on the property known as the Block House. This historic home, erected over a hundred years ago, was the property of the late Mr. and Mrs. John Reiley [sic]. And upon her death last July, Mrs. Reiley [sic], who had inherited it from her mother, left it to nine nieces and nephews. [List of heirs.] They in turn, realizing the historic value of the place, have decided to turn it into a museum for the benefit of the public. The official opening is today.

This museum did not happen by chance. It was a mission that Margaret actively, intelligently, and aggressively pursued. The legal and purchasing expenses from the eight other heirs alone were considerable and the negotiations required great patience. Her hard work and tenacity, especially in view of her active philanthropic, social, and family life in Washington and the poor health of her husband, are very impressive.

Margaret quickly became an evangelist for her museum. She nurtured the

This photograph was staged to publicize the Fort Hunter Museum. Margaret Wister Meigs sits on the sofa.

interest of visitors by preaching Fort Hunter's history. She hired professional photographers and staged elaborate photo sessions, re-creating for the camera various romantic historic cameos to be used as publicity stills and postcards. She developed various logos, slogans, and printed materials to advertise Fort Hunter. Two often-used slogans—"Fort Hunter: Where Godey's Ladies Book comes to life" and "Fort Hunter: Where the Blue Mountains cross the Susquehanna"—traded on two attractions, the natural beauty of the site and the historic collection contained within the Mansion and buildings.

In opening the museum, Margaret had the opportunity to experiment in the creation of historical period rooms, using the many raw ingredients existing in the house from the various Reily and Meigs homes. Because of the overwhelming number of items from the second half of the nineteenth century, she decided that the interiors of the Mansion would reflect the early Victorian period. While this was a period of fond memories for Margaret and there were few museums dedicated to this era at the time, pragmatism more likely prompted her decision. Victorian items were out of fashion and not yet recognized as valuable, so Margaret could afford to fill voids in her collection of Victorian period antiques at a reasonable cost. It was only as recently as the 1980s that the true value of her remarkable collection has been comprehended. Much from these early museum interiors are what remain in the Mansion today.

On November 5, 1940, Dr. Edward Browning Meigs died of the tuberculosis that had plagued him for eleven years. The death of her husband clearly left a void in Margaret's life, a void perhaps filled with the continuing demands of the Fort Hunter property and her many

activities. The onset of World War II and the opening of Fort Indiantown Gap, an army training center about ten miles east of Fort Hunter, found Margaret and the property involved in the war effort. Red Cross classes were offered at Fort Hunter, and the old Tavern House and stables were hastily renovated into apartments for the wives of officers stationed nearby. The museum was closed, and those rooms were also rented out. The end of the war in 1945 allowed for the eventual return to a bustling normalcy at the property, and the Mansion museum re-opened. A housing shortage after the war permitted the continued use of the old Tavern House as apartments to help generate modest income for the property.

In 1954, at age seventy-two, Margaret suffered a stroke. Travel became very difficult, and visits to her beloved Fort Hunter were now rare. Her attendance at the marriage of Arthur, her oldest son, to Ellen Lee Blackwell in Richmond, Virginia, on February 12, 1955, caused concern. When the driver arrived to pick up Margaret at her home during a snowstorm, he asked if she still wanted to make the trip. The feisty Margaret replied, "I now want, more than ever, to make the trip!"

While visiting her summer home in Woods Hole, Massachusetts, on July 16, 1955, Margaret revised her will with two codicils relating to the provisions for the Fort Hunter property, giving seventy-three acres and $50,000 to the newly created nonprofit Fort Hunter Foundation. "I have full confidence that the Directors, Officers and Advisors of said corporation will utilize said legacy wisely, bearing in mind my keen and most sincere interest in maintaining Fort Hunter Museum for its great cultural and historical value." The first directors of the foundation were Margaret; her four children, Arthur, Wister, Mary, and Sarah; her sister's daughter

Master bedroom of the Fort Hunter Mansion in the 1930s. Much of the interior of the Mansion from this period remains today.

Sarah Logan Starr Blain; and another relative, locally prominent Harrisburg attorney Spencer G. Hall. Assets were valued at $45,000 in real and personal property. The intention of the foundation was to carry out Margaret Wister Meigs's "living museum" concept by mixing furnishings and other items in various rooms in much the same manner that a family would accumulate various items through continuously occupying the same gracious home. At the time, Dr. Wister Meigs, Margaret's son, pointed out that rooms devoted to displays represented a blending of some very good collection items with everyday things that went into making up a "comfortable high middle class home of the late 18th and early 19th centuries."

Realizing the importance of the local Harrisburg community to the perpetuity of Margaret's vision, at the meeting of the foundation on May 23, 1956, "it was suggested a membership organization to be known as 'Friends of Fort Hunter' be formed to spread wider information on what is happening at the Museum." This organization was officially created "for the express purpose of making 'Fort Hunter Museum an educational, historical, cultural and social center for the people of this area and to assist in preserving and developing the property in order to promote community interest in this historic French and Indian distribution center.'" Its members would be the local stewards for the property. On August 25, 1957, the first annual Fort Hunter Day was held.

One year later, Margaret Wister Meigs died on June 2, 1958, at her home on M Street in Washington. Her ashes were buried alongside her husband in Devon, Pennsylvania. It was requested that tokens of sympathy be made in the form of contributions to the Fort Hunter Foundation. On Fort Hunter Day in 1960, her four children placed a memorial to Margaret on the property. Located in the center of the drive in front of the

Mansion, it is made of bricks from her then recently demolished home in Washington and contains a birdbath and a tile-lined niche. The handmade tiles, by noted ceramist Henry Varnum Poore, are said to depict the story of Margaret's life.

While concerned members of the foundation continued to oversee the property from a distance, dedicated local Friends of Fort Hunter volunteers carried Fort Hunter through the 1960s and 1970s. Keeping a constant eye toward placing the property with a public entity, which both parties believed could best guarantee the museum's future and existence, they developed large-scale restoration plans. They then began fulfilling those plans by fixing their sights on the Mansion House itself, centerpiece of the museum and property. While avoiding the huge problem of multiple large and decaying buildings, they hosted innumerable events that constantly kept the property in the newspaper and the public eye. They personally set about restoring rooms in the Mansion, sacrificing their time to do labor-intensive work.

The determination of specific Friends to maintain Fort Hunter's integrity became stronger. Over the years, many plans had been put forth to turn the property over to the care of a long-term agency. By the summer of 1978, the property had fallen on hard times. To visitors, the property held an eerie despondency that also had a romantic and melancholy quality about it.

In 1979, the opening of the limited-access Route 22/322, which circumvented the property, alleviated the almost impossible traffic on Front Street through the center of the historic estate. While the old River Road, known by various names through the years, had brought the possibility of a visiting pub-

The Tavern House in 1979, when deferred maintenance had taken it toll on the Fort Hunter buildings.

lic for the museum, it had also become a liability. Too many cars passed Fort Hunter, making it nothing but a visual landmark alongside a traffic jam. The sale of a portion of the Fort Hunter land for the construction of the new bypass supplied funds for a face-lift of the exterior of the Mansion. The house was repainted in its sparkling Colonial Revival scheme of cream and maroon, which remains today. Once again the Mansion looked like the gem it was.

After five years of careful and prolonged negotiations, on June 15, 1980, during an outdoor ceremony, thirty-eight acres, the buildings, their contents, and the endowment fund were transferred from the Fort Hunter Foundation to the county of Dauphin, by indenture. The foundation was dissolved, and a new board of trustees was created to manage the historic assets, ten acres, and the endowment. The remaining twenty-eight acres were given outright to the Dauphin County Parks and Recreation Department to be maintained as a park. Fort Hunter thus became the first developed park owned by the Dauphin County.

Many saw the creation of Fort Hunter Park as a consolidator for the county. Peter's Mountain geographically separates the rural northern area of Dauphin County from the urban southern portion. Fort Hunter was ideally located between the two and could serve all the people of the county. The Friends of Fort Hunter remained a constant during the transfer, with the added role of representation on the board of trustees. The goals of all parties involved had finally been realized. The property would be preserved for public use in perpetuity.

Margaret Wister Meigs and her dreams of a museum at Fort Hunter are a very important chapter in the history of the property. Her unique vision and early single-handed preservation efforts

The first lady of Pennsylvania, Ginny Thornburgh, presided over the ceremony donating Fort Hunter to the citizens of Dauphin County, 1980. County Commissioners, from left to right, are Stephen Reed, Norman Hetrick, and Jack Minnich.
COURTESY OF DAUPHIN COUNTY HISTORICAL SOCIETY

are laudable. The donation of the property to a government entity ended 110 years of ownership by the Boas family and its descendants.

In 1985, Dr. John Wister Meigs donated the 153-acre Fort Hunter Conservancy to the Board of Trustees for Fort Hunter. Known during the Reily era as the Chuckey Hill Tract, this piece of Fort Hunter property was the farthest from the Mansion House when the property was at its largest at the turn of the century. This significant gift was seen by many as a tangible vote of confidence in the new ownership and management of Fort Hunter.

Throughout these years, the collections in the buildings were consolidated, and a startling discovery was made. Much of Margaret's museum remained intact. Cupboards, drawers, and whole areas in the third floor had remained untouched for years, some boxes, trunks, and corners for as long as eighty years. A strong preservation philosophy began to develop. Because these objects had remained intact on the property for so long, their preservation for future generations became imperative. Particularly large collections included clothing, photographs, and the paper archives.

With these discoveries, the later years in the history of the property gained greater importance. The roles that the Reily, Boas, and Meigs families had played locally, regionally, statewide, and nationally were better understood. The physical alterations that these families had wrought upon the Fort Hunter lands were significant and irreversible. They, too, needed to figure into the history and interpretation of the property. On April 17, 1991, the mission of the museum was expanded and officially adopted by the Board of Trustees to read, in part, that the "Trustees seek to preserve the mansion and its lands so as to historically interpret the period 1720 to the present." Because of this refocused mission, the goal of the museum has been the preservation of the buildings and the collections. Under this philosophy, the interpretation is able to reflect all of the interesting layers of the history of the site.

Today the future of Fort Hunter looks better than ever. With the generous sustenance of the county commissioners, the fiduciary authority of the Board of Trustees for Fort Hunter, the enthusiasm and support of the Friends of Fort Hunter, and the professional direction of a stable staff, great things are happening.

Fort Hunter has a wealth of history that admirably reflects America's past. For almost every movement in the history of this nation, a reverberation was felt on this piece of land. This impressive resource can be used to educate residents, school groups, and tourists through a host of diverse and creative ways of both the history of Fort Hunter and the nation.

Visiting the Mansion and Park

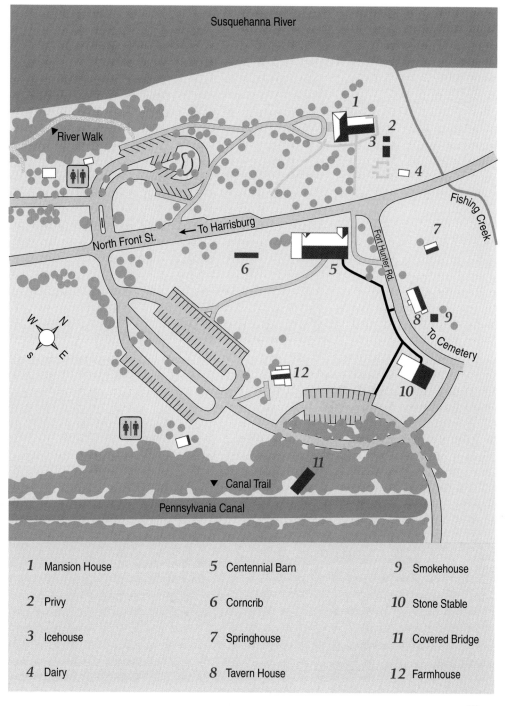

1	Mansion House	*5*	Centennial Barn	*9*	Smokehouse
2	Privy	*6*	Corncrib	*10*	Stone Stable
3	Icehouse	*7*	Springhouse	*11*	Covered Bridge
4	Dairy	*8*	Tavern House	*12*	Farmhouse

1 MANSION HOUSE

Sitting high and aloof on a bluff along the Susquehanna, the Mansion House at Fort Hunter has a commanding presence. Front Street, or the River Road, as it was historically known, has always separated the elegant Mansion House and its outbuildings and gardens from the rougher work of the farm on the other side of the road.

What is now a twenty-room house began in 1786 as a large two-room, two-story stone cabin. This solidly constructed home, with plenty of windows to provide a bright and airy interior, is the oldest structure on the property and forms the center portion in the rear of the Mansion today. As originally constructed, it had two multipurpose rooms on each floor and one massive fireplace on the first floor.

PHOTO BY CARL SOCOLOW ↓

In 1814, Archibald McAllister added an elegant Federal-style structure to the south of his original stone cabin. The stone cabin became a service ell on his grand new home. With a total of twelve rooms on three floors, eleven-foot-high ceilings, wide halls, a raised cellar, six-foot-tall windows, an elegant fanlight over the front door, and a classical Palladian window on the second floor, McAllister built a home without parallel in the area. Interior features such as light and fashionable trims and mantles, folding interior shutters on the second floor, elegantly paneled doors, fine brass hardware, and a cantilevered elliptical staircase set the house apart. Life in this house was architecturally prescribed to be far more formal than that in the old stone cabin.

47

The year 1870 saw a change in ownership of the property to the Boas family and changes to the by-then old and unfashionable Mansion House. As the owner of a finished lumbermill, Daniel Dick Boas used readily available stock to update the exterior of the Mansion House with a new cornice, heavy molding over each window, and a deep, rich color scheme of brown, maroon, and cream. With the addition of a new front porch, these alterations modernized the outside of the house in the more fashionable Italian Villa style. At the rear of the house, the Summer Kitchen was built—possibly to replace an earlier structure—and minor interior alterations were made. The parlor woodwork was also updated at this time, and the mantel was exchanged for a new one made of marble.

Under the Reily occupation of the Mansion House, alterations were minor. Regular redecoration kept the interiors fresh and fashionable. An awareness of America's historic architecture at the beginning of the twentieth century manifested itself in the replacement of the front porch with one of Colonial Revival design, the removal of all of the heavy hoods over the windows, with the exception of the one over the Palladian window, and a lighter color scheme. All of these alterations are preserved today. This building has been well maintained throughout its long life and has required only cosmetic restoration.

2 PRIVY

This Privy, or outhouse, was constructed around 1900. It was donated and moved here from the town of Matamoras, about five miles north of Fort Hunter, in 1985. The location and form of the original Mansion Privy, short for private, is unknown.

3 ICEHOUSE

Probably built around 1814, this specialized building was necessary for the preservation of foods through cooling. Before the widespread availability of mechanical cooling systems invented in 1913, food was purchased daily at the market. A plantation the size of Fort Hunter required the greater flexibility that an icehouse allowed. In the winter, ice was cut from a nearby millpond on the property, hauled to the Icehouse, placed down in the ground under the roof (the inside room extends three feet below grade), and packed with sawdust or straw for insulation. With good management, this ice would last until the next winter.

During the Boas renovations of 1870, the Icehouse received its elaborate cornice with paired Italianate brackets to match the Mansion House. The paired brackets were removed during a 1970s' restoration.

4 DAIRY

A plantation the size of Fort Hunter had many ancillary buildings necessary to the running of the property. While most were modest wood structures and have been lost, Fort Hunter is lucky to have retained many rare building types built in a substantial manner. The Dairy is a prime example.

Butter and cheese were luxury items, the production of which required a fickle process. The areas in this building were used for separating cream from milk, hanging up cheeses in muslin to drain, and storing home-churned butter. The timing of these processes and the temperature of the work area required extremely careful management. Attention to hygiene was vital.

The Dairy faces north to assure a constant cool temperature. It is accessible from two levels. Its location along the old River Road announced to passersby the elegance and status of the adjoining household. According to an 1835 description of the Fort Hunter Dairy from *The Cultivator*:

The interior of the house, principally under ground, was fitted up with cistern, in which water stood nearly to the tops of the pans of milk, which were arranged in them. For want of a natural spring, which many Pennsylvanians consider almost indispensable in a milk house, the water was

PHOTO BY CARL DICKSON

conducted in a pipe from the well-pump, and after filling the cisterns to a certain height, passed off at the opposite side. The object was to obtain a cool temperature, in the heat of summer, which greatly facilitates the separation of the cream from the milk, and this abject [sic] was amply effected, with the labor of working occasionally at the well-pump.

This building was in ruin during much of the twentieth century, with only the three walls built into the hill remaining more or less intact. The building as it stands now is the result of one of the few conjectural restorations at Fort Hunter. It was rebuilt in 1998 and, like the other buildings on the property, looks like an early-nineteenth-century outbuilding updated in 1870 with a heavy Italianate cornice and color scheme.

5 CENTENNIAL BARN

Built in 1876, the centennial year of the founding of the United States, this massive building makes a powerful statement on the property. Placed in the middle of all the buildings at Fort Hunter, it can be seen from every direction and is one of the newest structures on the estate. Viewed from the Mansion and Front Street, it acts as a screen to hide the hard work of the farm. From the farm side of the property, it is readily accessible and the center of all activity. This barn was built to house a budding dairy operation, which delivered, with a fleet of its own wagons, fresh milk to the residents of Harrisburg. It was built with the most up-to-date facilities that took into consideration scientific farming techniques using rather modern time and movement studies. During the life of the operations as a dairy, the facilities were continually upgraded.

The exterior of the building was built to impress. With Gothic Revival details in its pinnacles, quatrefoil bargeboards, and heavy drip moldings over the windows, it strongly resembles a church. This effect is further carried to the roof, with its huge, spire-like ventilator. Originally, two miniature versions of the main cupola flanked it and would have provided a spectacular silhouette against the sky.

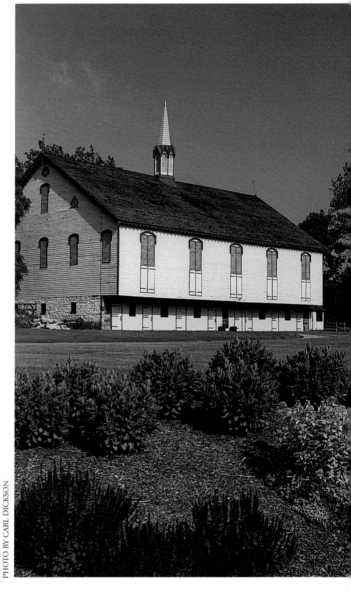

PHOTO BY CARL DICKSON

The restoration of this well-constructed building in 1985 required a new roof and a restored paint scheme. The first floor was modernized in 1987 to provided comfortable program, exhibit, and meeting spaces.

6 CORNCRIB

Probably built around the same time as the Centennial Barn (1876), this structure has been through various incarnations. It is built on stilts to keep out hungry rodents and has slat sides for ventilation. Its overhanging roof and inward-slanting walls protected the contents from the ele-ments. During harvest time, hinged panels high in the slat west wall could be opened and corn, shucked but still on the cob, could be dumped in from wagons. For feeding, the door on the north end opened, and corn could be shoveled out.

In 1985, it was moved from a more central location in the barnyard to its present location, and a performance stage was built in front of it.

PHOTO BY CARL DICKSON

7 SPRINGHOUSE

Built to protect the spring from contamination, the Springhouse also served as a place to keep vegetables and fruits from the garden and orchard cool, along with barrels and jugs of cider and vinegar. With Archibald McAllister's whiskey operations, brandies might have been stored here as well. During the later era of the Fort Hunter Dairy, milk was stored here, along with the mechanical cream separator. Containing two rooms, each with a stone staircase leading down to a stone trough with a constantly running water supply, this building remains cool on the hottest of days.

This building has a long history of losing its roof. Because of its location in a low-lying area, any flooding of the river backs up Fishing Creek and gently lifts the roof off the stone structure. In 1999, Hurricane Hugo swept through the park, and an enormous sycamore tree fell and crushed the roof. It was restored in 2000 with an exaggerated cornice in keeping with Boas's remodeling of the property in 1870.

8 TAVERN HOUSE

While at first this building may appear quite simple, it has, in fact, evolved into its present form through many changes. The workhorse of the property, this building has seen heavy use over the years. Each use wrought its own alterations, so that today the Tavern House has many stories to tell.

This house began life as a small stone two-story building with two fireplaces, one on each floor. It was about 23 feet wide, 23 feet deep, and 25 feet to the ridge. It was constructed sometime in the eighteenth century, and while little of this early structure remains today, it is perhaps the oldest building on the property. It is assumed to be the earliest form of the operating Tavern House.

Around 1810, with increasing wealth and general prosperity, Archibald McAllister made an addition to his old tavern. A much larger, taller, and airier building, this addition left the original building in its shadow. Consisting of a large room and hall on the first floor, three bedrooms on the second floor, and an unfinished attic, it has the floor plan of a town house in a city. A single door on the first floor connected it to the old house to the east. Because of the different floor heights of the second floors of these attached buildings, there was no access between the two sides on the second floor.

Until 1870, the Tavern House presented a rather lopsided facade to the public. Its uses were equally varied and picturesque. It began life as a tavern, but later it was used by a son as a home and it was also rented out to tenants. With the purchase of the property in 1870 by Daniel Dick Boas and the full-scale remodeling taking place on the other buildings at Fort Hunter, the old Tavern House came under scrutiny. Apparently the original eighteenth-century portion of the house was deemed unsalvageable, for it was demolished. But because the 1810 addition was built on top of the fireplace wall of the eighteenth-century structure, that wall with its fireplaces and the cellar below had to remain. Today they give the necessary clues to conjecture the size and appearance of the original building.

After the demolition of the eighteenth-century portion of the house, in 1870 a new structure went up in its place. Though constructed of wood, it matched the remaining 1810 house in size and scale and presented the symmetrical facade seen on the building today. A one-story addition placed across the rear of the Tavern House around 1900 was removed during restoration. This building was heavily used over the years and required a major restoration, completed in 1997.

9 SMOKEHOUSE

A smokehouse was another important structure on a farm. It was built solely for the preservation of meats. Meat was first cured in brine for six to eight weeks. After being hung in the smokehouse, a smoldering fire was lit under it. Different woods on the fire gave the meat different flavors. Meat was smoked from one day to a week, depending on its size. Many wooden smokehouses and their contents were lost because untended fires crept to the sides of the buildings and ignited the structures. Perhaps that was the fate of the original smokehouse here, because the current structure is a restoration built in 1998 on the original foundation and based on old photographs.

PHOTO BY CARL DICKSON

57

10 STONE STABLE

The Stone Stable is a rare survivor of an English-type drive-through barn. Constructed around 1810, the Stable is different from most barns in the area, such as the nearby Centennial Barn, which were built in the German tradition into a hill. This provided ground-level access to two levels of the building and was very practical. The Stone Stable, on the other hand, is accessible from one level only and required heavy lifting through exterior doors to get hay and grains into the second-floor storage area. The use of this English form is in keeping with its builder Archibald McAllister's Scots heritage.

This elegantly simple building remained empty for many years. Heavy snows in 1994 caused the roof and east wall to collapse. The Stone Stable received a major restoration in 1998, and today the second floor houses a climate-controlled museum storage facility, while the first floor is used for program space. Surprisingly, it retains one complete row of its original horse stalls along the west wall.

11 COVERED BRIDGE (FUTURE RESTORATION)

The Covered Bridge is not original to the Fort Hunter property. Called the Everhart Bridge, it was built around 1870 and spanned Little Buffalo Creek in Perry County on the west side of the Susquehanna River. It came to Fort Hunter through the early preservation efforts of Margaret Wister Meigs in 1941.

As a child, Meigs's parents owned and ran the Duncannon Iron Works. She undoubtedly knew this bridge in her youth. Later, when she heard of its planned replacement, she purchased it for $70 and moved it to the front lawn of the Mansion House. "I bought it simply to preserve it," she said at the time.

This bridge uses the multiple king post truss system and is typical of the simply constructed covered bridges built throughout Pennsylvania at the time.

12 FARMHOUSE

This charming cottage, with board-and-batten siding, looks like it could have been built in the nineteenth century. In fact, Margaret Wister Meigs had it inexpensively constructed in the 1940s, along with another nearby house that was since demolished. This house received a major renovation in 1980. Today a family that provides on-site security lives here.

PHOTO BY CARL DICKSON

For information on hours, tours, programs, and activities at
Fort Hunter Mansion and Park, visit **www.forthunter.org**.

About the Author

Carl A. Dickson has been the director of Fort Hunter Mansion and Park for nearly two decades. He lives in Harrisburg, Pennsylvania.